TO: Phelena Hughes

The
Recipe
Have a Seat at Our Table...

Remembering America's
Traditions

Enjoy!

11/11/06

Annette Marie Council

Annette Council

The Recipe
Have a Seat at Our Table...

For information address:
NP Press
P. O. Box 4713
Chapel Hill, NC 27515
919-259-2481
www.annettecouncil.com

THE COVER—Author Annette Council and her family on the front steps of their home on Easter Sunday, 1961.
L-R: Mama Dip, Bon, Bill, Norma Frances, Lane, Spring, Neecy, Yea-Yea, Joe Nathan

Cover Photo by Roland Giduz
Cover Graphics and Design by Connie Carley
Book Layout and Design by Sara and Stewart Sanders
Portrait of Author by Ann Jacoby

ISBN: 0-9773959-1-X

Library of Congress Control Number: 2005936595

Printed in the United States of America

Dedication

In memory of my daddy, Joe "Tight Rope" Council who inspired me to be what God would have me to be, and I will always remember him as one great cook.

June 24, 1924–September 21, 2003

Acknowledgements

I am grateful to a number of people who have helped shape my life experiences and therefore made this book possible. I first give thanks to God for allowing this birthing process to take place at this time in my life.

I thank you, Mildred "Mama Dip" Council, because of who you are and what I have learned from you. Your dream was the inspiration that made this book possible—teaching me that blessings are received as one confronts life challenges.

To Mary Glen Benton, who asked me, "Why don't you write a book and tell your story about the legacy of your family?" Thanks for your suggestion that gave me the vision and confidence that I could really do this.

Special thanks to my brothers (Roy, Geary, Joe, and William) and sisters (Norma, Julia, Sandra, and Anita) with whom I have spent most of my life. This book speaks of you often; we are a major part of the ingredients in our family's recipe that Mama used to become successful.

I thank my daughter Millen who assisted me when I needed help, cheered me on from start to finish, and allowed me to share her computer to write this book.

To Ann Jacoby for being my right hand whenever I needed you. Your inspiration, dedication, and friendship have helped me in more ways than I can express during this process. Thanks for hanging in there with me, girl!

To Jason and Jacob Jacoby, thank you for your patience while your mom took time away from home to assist me with preparation of my manuscript.

To Rev. Dr. Junious Jones, thanks so much for the countless hours that you spent with me on this project. Your constructive criticism and fruitful suggestions encouraged me to add more flavor, as a result making *The Recipe* more colorful.

A special thanks to my readers (Roland Giduz, Suzan Johnson, Millen Umoh, Patrick Kelly, and Tamara O'Briant) who taught me how to develop better writing skills.

To my high school gym teacher, Susan McDonald, with whom I've had a lasting relationship, and at the end of this project you helped me cross my "T's" and dot my "I's." You're a treasure, thank you so much!

In loving memory of my sixth grade teacher, Mrs. Lucille McDougle who helped me to understand that my integration experience would be a gradual and rewarding transition.

Thanks to my twelfth grade teacher, Mrs. Geraldine Young who encouraged me to become an accountant as she saw my potential.

I personally thank the media (*New York Times, Southern Living Magazine, GQ Magazine,* "Good Morning America," Food Network, Sara Moulton, QVC, UNC-TV, *Chapel Hill Herald, Chapel Hill Newspaper, News & Observer, The Daily Tarheel,* and all others) who thought enough of my family to seek us out of the crowd and acknowledge our success. Because of you we have customers throughout the United States.

I thank each and every customer who patronized our businesses throughout the years (1963–present). You were and still today are a huge part of our success. Thanks also for believing that our products are worthy of your hard-earned dollars, and for supporting our tremendous growth, much of which has occurred from you passing on a good word to others.

There is a special place in my heart that belongs to each of you. Thanks again to all of you!

Contents

Preface

Often I'm asked, "Are you one of Mama Dip's daughters?" Some continue to ask how I manage so well in doing what I do and remain both physically and spiritually sound. After pondering this question for quite some time, I realized that most of my life has been spent living my mama's dream. Because of this, I became curious and decided to tell my story. I felt I needed to challenge my life's struggles so that the spirit God placed inside of me would manifest, thus allowing me to enjoy life to its fullest.

My story, *The Recipe*, is about how I came to live my dream. It contains the challenges and struggles my family endured as we went from "neighborhood bonding" to building successful enterprises in our community. My grandparents were Daddy's and Mama's guides; in turn Daddy and Mama were guides for me and my brothers and sisters. Now as we look back we all are amazed at what was made possible.

The Recipe is a very personal story. It's about surviving when there is not enough, maintaining when there is just enough, and remembering where we came from when there is more than enough.

In creating *The Recipe*, I have included what I consider my family's list of ingredients for growth. Using these ingredients, I created a recipe that I consider to be inspirational and useful in the daily lives of those who seek guidance. Guidance is what made my mama a very successful woman, and I can now say it was her guidance that inspired me to write this book.

In writing *The Recipe*, I recognized the domino-effect of accomplishing a dream. Let me elaborate a little about three of "Mama Dip's" dreams. As a young child she planted pumpkin seeds. When it was time to harvest her crop she knew that her mission was accomplished; three lovely pumpkins. As an adult she planted her seeds of wisdom in soils of communities. She feels that the importance of family and the traditions of America must continue, therefore another mission was accomplished. Later in her life, she planted a financial seed in the amount of $64 to start her own restaurant business. Again another mission was accomplished. A successful restaurant business now in its 29th year was established, which made "Mama Dip" well-known in her community and nationwide.

My story, *The Recipe*, is about our family of eight children, a cousin who became my brother, a Mama with a dream, and a Daddy with the heart to hustle who was around for as long as he could endure.

Introduction

According to my birth certificate I was born February 17, 1956 at 5:57am, a nine-pound, six-ounce, Negro baby girl, the seventh of eight children born to Joe and Mildred Council. My family lived in the heart of Chapel Hill, North Carolina. At the time of my birth, Daddy was 31 years old and Mama was 26. They already had six children with three still in diapers. My parents named me Annette Marie Council and nicknamed me "Neecy." Later on in my life, when I questioned my nickname, I asked Mama, "Why ya'll call me Neecy?" She explained they called me Neecy because in black families the second from the last child was sometimes called the "knee baby."

Others in my family were also given nicknames—Spring (Anita's middle name), Bill (short for William), Yea-Yea (Geary), Bon (Julia), and Lane (Sandra)— but not Norma Frances and Joe Nathan; they were called by their first and middle names. Nicknames have been common in the black community for generations.

I never knew my mama's parents, Ed and Effie Cotten, since they had passed away before I was born. Fortunately, I was surrounded by their siblings, my uncles and aunts, on a daily basis. I was raised around the corner from Daddy's stepfather, William, and his mother, Mary Minor. Daddy was the only child. He always reminded me how much I looked like his maternal grandmother, Martha Ann. Folks around town called me "Mary Minor" because of my resemblance to my grandmother. When they were not calling me "Mary Minor" they were calling me "Dip" as they would the rest of my brothers and sisters. Mama earned her nickname "Dip" from her siblings when she was growing up. When Mama was young there was a large barrel kept on her family's porch that caught rain water. She has always been very tall with long arms. When the water was low the other children watched as Mama was the only child who could reach way down deep into the barrel and dip the water out. I am used to being called several different names in my life, but I've always preferred to be called by my birth name, Annette.

Nearly every day of my life, I watched as Mama worked day in and day out, sometimes working three jobs to get to the wonderful place that she is in her life today. I now know that she was creating recipes for a successful restaurant business. Every day was a work day except when she was sick. She was employed at both fraternity and sorority houses, and on the University of North Carolina campus. Mama also worked many years for Roland Giduz (former vice-mayor of Chapel Hill) and his family, providing domestic duties—cooking, cleaning, and caring for their children. Mama learned from the many people whom she encountered daily. She observed her surroundings, taking note of the things that she could incorporate into making life better for her family.

My family never experienced poverty. Daddy and Mama never spoke to us about it. Mama says, "Life is not about what you don't have, but what you have," and, "Life is not about where you are, but where you are going." My parents made the best of what they had. We always had good hot food, good clothes, shoes, and a house with a bathroom. They made sure that our family was comfortable and our needs were met.

Mama was the only homemaker that I knew who worked outside the home. I consider Mama a warrior, with the steadfastness of an oak tree that nurtured acorns of children, whether they belonged to her or not, but surrounded her every day. She loved them all, filled their bellies, gave them words of wisdom, and there was always a "welcome mat." Like she still says, "It takes a community (village) to raise children," long before it became politically popular to state. Mama's platform in life is what mattered most to her—and that is what she has always preached—the importance of family and community. Realizing that it takes a community to raise a child, she became active in the black neighborhoods surrounding our family.

Back in the early sixties Daddy's parents built a restaurant in their backyard. Their venture took place when blacks weren't allowed to have much at all, and their business was successful for over twenty years. I remember walking around to my grandparent's house as a young girl to watch the construction workers, covered with dust from the mortar that was used to lay the bricks for the restaurant's foundation. Soon after its completion, Daddy began working there, even though his primary job was at Coleman's Lumber Company as a laborer. Daddy made time to work at the restaurant part-time where he learned to cut whole chickens into parts.

Adding to her list of jobs, Mama also began to work at my grandparents' restaurant in her spare time as a short-order cook. Cooking was her opportunity to show off her gifts and to enjoy the things that she had loved to do since she was nine years old. Most of my family worked at the restaurant when they were old enough. All I was accustomed to was loose change that my grandparents paid me for doing small chores for them. After I discovered that some of my brothers and sisters were getting paid with dollars, I too wanted to work and make more money. I was eager to know what it felt like to make dollars and not just loose change. I didn't get a chance to work in the restaurant because I was too young. After my grandparents' retirement, Daddy and Mama continued their legacy. That's when I got my chance to work for dollars.

Mama inspired her children at a young age to be mentally tough as we watched her go about her daily routine. No matter what challenges life had coming the world would keep on going. She proved by working numerous jobs and raising nine children that we must "keep on keeping it on." She also taught us that what we learned and accomplished in our lives would help build our character. Mama once said to me, "Neecy, you gotta dig a little deeper down in your soul in order to understand the meaning of self, so that you can inspire others," as she had done. She then would tell me, "No matter what the struggle is now, down the road it will get better, but not always easier."

I was inspired to write this book by a deep desire to share the story about the history of my family. I am grateful to be a part of my family that successfully achieved its dreams through generations. I am sharing my story so that you may be inspired to write yours, and I believe that everybody has a story to tell. "Come on in and have a seat at our table!"

At the end of each section, you'll receive an "ingredient" that my family strives to incorporate in our daily lives, and to create our recipe for successful experiences. Our lives have inspired many and I hope our story is the guidance that motivates you to create success in your life by using "The Recipe."

Making the Best of Meager Beginnings

I remember back to the time when I was a young child, four years old, frail, and tall. I remember this distinctly because this is when I learned my multiplication tables. I could easily count by fives and tens very fast. I'd stand in the middle of the floor in my dusty shorts, ashy knees, flip flops, and count. I was on showcase every time one of Daddy's or Mama's friends came over to visit. Mama sat on the couch as her smile gave me the applause that boosted my confidence. She'd say, "Show 'em what you kin do Neecy," and I began reciting one number after the other standing proudly and confidently. Everyone stared at me as I counted, "Five, ten, fifteen, twenty..." and then, "Ten, twenty, thirty, forty..." in the living room of this big old house that we lived in. After I finished counting, everybody clapped, and I fell back on the couch beside Mama with my shy smile.

Most weekends around our house were a busy scene. A typical Saturday unfolded with my brothers, sisters, and me eating bowls of Colonial store brand frosted flakes, while we watched Bugs Bunny and the Flintstones. In the front of the

TV we were lined up on our bellies, holding our heads up with our hands, and our elbows were touching the cold linoleum floor. Mama was working at one of her domestic jobs or "fixin" ladies' hair in our kitchen. Daddy would just be getting home from being out all night gambling. He expected the house to be cleaned on Saturday morning. Of course, being like most kids, we didn't start cleaning the house and doing our chores before he came home.

We were always on the lookout, listening for the rumble of his car pulling up in the driveway. At the sound of the car door closing, everybody jumped up and yelled, "Here come Daddy!" We all started running, often running right smack into each other grabbing the broom or whatever we could find to make it look as if we were already cleaning the house. We struggled with each other for possession of the mop, broom and dust rag. As we scattered about we sometimes ended up yelling at each other. "Move out of my way!" We also knew the sound of his footsteps. As soon as Daddy walked in the front door he began hollering at us for not having the house clean. The surprised look on our faces proved to him that we had not been cleaning. Daddy never opened his mouth to speak—he gritted his teeth and puckered his lips whenever he talked or yelled at us. The first thing he'd say when entering the house was, "Cut that TV off, get your damn ass up and start cleaning this house!" He loosened his belt; however, he rarely used it, given that he knew his presence was the key. Most of the whuppin' was left up to Mama, and boy she never ran out of energy. At our house nobody got out of house work and nine children were always on duty to clean up.

My brothers got their haircuts at Perry's barber shop on Graham Street after helping clean the house. They were not always happy about getting haircuts. The bubble gum machine sitting close to the front door was the most exciting part. They took their pennies and used every single one to get as many gumballs as possible.

When they entered the barber shop there was always a warm welcome from Joyce, who cut their hair. She was the only woman barber in town. My brothers feared the clippers, and sometimes she accidentally nicked their necks and ears. When it was Bill's turn, he had to remove his eyeglasses while the barber palmed his head as if it was a basketball. She then pushed his head from side to side and held down his ears until she was done. My brothers were always glad when they got back home to look in the mirror to see their well-groomed heads. I didn't know what it was like to get a haircut, but it couldn't have been worse than what my sisters and I experienced getting our hair straightened with a hot comb.

The barber shop was behind our house, through a small alley next to the Laundromat, which is where my sisters and I spent countless hours washing and folding clothes for our family. When we went to the Laundromat we had piles of clothes for eleven family members. Customers unloading their cars and entering the Laundromat were always on the lookout, especially when they saw my family hauling bag after bag of clothes, dragging them to the washing machines lined against the wall—to claim them. They often tried to rush and beat us inside to claim washing machines so they would not have to wait a long time.

When Mama got off work she washed the girls' hair one after another in the kitchen sink. When it was my turn, I stood in front of the sink to hang my head under the faucet. She then poured on the shampoo using her long fingers to scrub my scalp until it hurt. Then she grabbed a jelly jar from the cabinet and filled it with warm water. She used it to rinse the suds off of the hairline at the back of my neck, since my head couldn't reach the faucet. Sometimes I had to stand on my tip-toes while water ran on my hair.

While Mama poured the water from the jar onto my head, water got in my ears, and I tried to turn my head the other way to empty them. She quickly hollered, "Be still!" I couldn't hear anything because of the water in my ears until after she was done; then a towel was tossed over my head. I grabbed the towel, wrapped it tightly around my head, and squeezed as much of the water out of my hair as I could so that water did not run down my neck or get into my eyes. Standing up, I'd shake my head until the water was out of my ears, and then it was the next sister's turn.

After getting our hair washed we played around the house most of the day not going too far away. In the evening after our hair had air dried and was kinky and matted, Mama yelled, "C'mon Neecy!" so that she could straighten my hair using a hot comb. None of us wanted to go first, but we were eager for the process to be over. We had to sit down between her legs on a tiny stool, or sometimes on a clothes basket filled with clean, folded clothes until she was done. Occasionally, I had to lay my head on Mama's lap while I concentrated on her penny loafers, trying to divert my attention from the oncoming hot comb. An electric hot plate was used to heat the comb. When the comb was hot she wiped it across an old wet rag sitting next to the hot plate to release some of the heat. The burst of steam went straight up in the air and the crackling sizzle from the release of the heat was very scary to me—fear started to set in.

My brothers stood around and laughed at us making ugly faces. If I did not hold my head the way Mama wanted me to, she yelled, "Hold ya head up!" as she yanked my hair. Then I yelled, saying to my brothers, "Leave me alone!" In a stern voice, Mama told them, "Ya'll go head and take a bath right now!" If they did not move she yelled at them again, "Do ya'll hear me?" "Yeah Mama!" they'd say, and they went to take their baths. My brothers always teased my sisters and me until we cried. We were glad Mama ran the boys off because we didn't need any distractions.

Mama began sectioning my hair with a comb as she struggled to get through my kinky hair. With her right hand she scooped a finger full of hair grease from the jar and wiped it on the back of her left hand. Section by section, she applied grease on my scalp. Once this was done, her right hand started toward my head, her left hand grabbed and yanked a patch of hair that she had sectioned off. I knew then that it was time for me not to move; with her tight grip on my hair my head wasn't going anywhere.

Mama was not aware of her own strength, but her grip wasn't the only thing that I feared. When the heat from the comb came in contact with my hair, I could hear the sizzling sound from the grease as well as from my hair not being completely dry. I quivered while trying to hold still when I felt the steam from the comb moving through my hair. The odor from the cooking hair was nearly indescribable, but it smelled somewhat like burning leaves. This smell lingered in the house for quite some time.

When it was time for treating the edges and the nape of my neck (called the kitchen), Mama had to get very close to my scalp and I jerked. Sometimes our skin was accidentally burned from being touched by the hot comb when we moved. I sat nervously. Sooner or later I flinched, cried, and yelled, "Ouch!" When I pulled away from Mama, she grabbed me by my shoulders and yanked me back while she hollered, "Sit down so I can finish!" Mama had no time for me jerking since she had four more heads to straighten. After she was done I went to the bathroom to put some Vaseline on the burn mark on my ear. Then I'd retreat somewhere in the house trying to control my sobbing and calm myself down.

Despite the weekly traumatic hair straightening process, I was happy as a lark to look through my tear-stained, hazel eyes in the mirror; and see my lovely bangs curled up on my forehead. We were like Mama's assembly line, one after the other for the entire process.

Mama used her beautician skills that she learned at the beauty school in Durham to create our hairdos. She knew that my sisters and I were happy when she made us bangs and sometimes hanging curls. Mama was determined that no other children in town were going to look better than hers. After a little while, still holding onto the jar of Vaseline, I tore off a piece of toilet paper that I had used to wipe my tears so that I could polish my black patent leather shoes. When I was done my shoes looked like they were brand new.

On Easter Sunday mornings I woke up to the smell of bacon and sausage frying. Sunday was a day that breakfast was like a full-course meal. Mama was in the kitchen with the heated oven door laid open while she placed slices of bread with pats of butter on a baking pan. When one side was toasted she flipped the hot bread over with her fingertips to toast the other side.

It took a lot of food to feed my family. Mama prepared a large pot of grits, and eighteen eggs were scrambled, often with cheese, in the same cast iron frying pan that was used to fry the bacon. She also added some of the bacon fat to add more flavor to the scrambled eggs. While the grits bubbled and splattered onto the stove top, Mama always kept her dish rag close by so that she could wipe up any mess on the stove.

When my brothers, sisters, and I got out of bed we began to prepare for Sunday school. We washed our faces and brushed our teeth. I rubbed my body with Vaseline, especially my legs and face so I would shine. When I sat down for breakfast I was dressed in my crinoline slip, ruffled anklet socks, shiny patent leather shoes, everything except for my pretty dress. My sisters were also dressed this way for breakfast. My brothers wore their tee-shirts, pants, socks, and shoes, but not their shirt and necktie. Mama was not about to let us mess up our outfits before we went to church; and as for me, I was not about to get a speck of dirt on myself, especially before Sunday school. I was Miss Prissy then and I still love to dress up.

We all gathered around the table to eat breakfast. The pot of grits sat on a dish towel that caught the drippings from around the sides of the pot. The cooked eggs were in a plastic bowl and the bacon, sausage, and toast in pie pans. There was never a breakfast in my house that did not include molasses and grape jelly. I loved and still love molasses, that's why I claim that the birth marks on my forehead and arms resemble the look of molasses dripping.

There was always a lot of commotion at our breakfast table. With everyone as hungry as could be, we hollered at each other, "Pass me the bread!" while some of us were reaching over one another to grab a piece of bacon. I said, "I don't want eggs." But I got them anyway. "Say the Grace," Mama yelled from the kitchen. Then my brothers, sisters, and I put our hands together, bowed our heads and a quick prayer was said.

I grabbed a plate from the stack and a fork from the pile that Mama set in the middle of the table. I sliced a pat of butter with my fork, mashed it together with molasses on my plate to make a buttery spread, then I drizzled it over my toast and made a molasses sandwich.

The majority of the time I was busy eating molasses when Mama approached the table and said, "Eat those eggs too!" I did not like eggs a lot and I thought that I was going to get away without eating them. Mama was on the lookout for plates that were not empty. Sometimes I'd add eggs to my molasses sandwich which made them taste pretty good.

After breakfast we had to wash our hands and faces again. Mama laid the girls' dresses across our bed, and the boys' shirts and neckties were hanging on the bathroom doorknob. I put on my new pink and white flowered dress with a big white collar. My dress had a big bow that tied in the back and my crinoline slip made my dress stand out. With my pretty dress, shiny shoes, and new hairdo, I knew that I was beautiful. While the girls were dressing, Mama tied my brothers' neckties and made sure they were wearing a belt.

Our house was located at 100 Merritt Mill Road in Chapel Hill, where it intersects with Carrboro. We attended Sunday school across the street from our house at St. Paul's Church. Reverend Duhart was the preacher. The Reverend was a jolly, tall, old man with very dark skin that always shined. He had a bald head and wore rimless glasses that sat just below his eyes. My brothers, sisters, and I tried to avoid him because he always grabbed our cheeks and squeezed them as hard as he could every time he came near us. This was his way of showing affection, but boy it hurt! Every Sunday was church day and the children in our house had to go to Sunday school. We always prepared for church on Saturday evenings.

Daddy never went to church since most of the time in the mornings he was asleep from being up all night playing

St. Paul's Church

poker. Mama rarely went to church since she was always cleaning, cooking and serving dinner for one of the white families that employed her. On special occasions and holidays she drove down to Hamlet Chapel Church, her family's church, to attend service.

Mama gave us ten cents each, a nickel for Sunday school and a nickel to spend at Blackburn's store. Sometimes we went to the milk dairy where most of the kids from neighboring churches gathered to get ice cream cones. I grabbed my patent leather pocket book with my old handkerchief tucked inside that Mama had given to each of the girls. We all darted out the front door, jumping over the dirt parts of the sidewalk so that our shiny shoes would not get dusty. My sisters and I held hands as we skipped across the street to church.

When we arrived at church, I hurried directly to the front and sat in the middle row of the second pew (my favorite seat). Before I sat down I reached behind me to smooth the back of my dress. Sitting down, I placed my long fingers and held onto the hem of my dress to spread the front out so that it did not get wrinkles. No one could sit close to me. I did not want my dress to get messed up in any way. After I was settled I looked up to see Reverend Duhart looking out into the congregation from the pulpit, remembering to stay clear for my jaw's sake. He wore a black robe, often looking over his glasses while watching as everyone was finding a place to sit.

The congregation waited patiently until it was time for Sunday school to begin. The teacher gathered all of the children and escorted them to their respective classes in the annex where she read the lesson aloud. She explained it to everyone and then gave each child a short sentence to recite about what we had learned. Afterwards, all of the classes gathered back into the sanctuary to present their lessons.

One by one each child had to stand in front of the congregation and recite their sentence. One Sunday when it was my turn to speak, I stood up and shuffled sideways until I made my way to the end of the pew. I slowly walked to the front and faced the congregation. By then, I noticed that more people had arrived early for the church service, which made me very nervous. I stared at the front door and wanted desperately to run. Nothing came out of my mouth when I tried to speak. I forgot what I was supposed to say and I was totally embarrassed. I hurried back to my seat with my head down, only glancing up to make sure that I didn't bump into anything and sat back down.

At the end of Sunday school my siblings and I ran around the corner from our house to the store. We went there almost every day when we had money. With our change we could buy a bag filled with 2ffers; Jack cookies, bubble gum, BB Bats, Sugar Daddies, Icicles or Push-Ups. We had five cents to spend on anything we wanted. After we returned home, we had to change out of our Sunday clothes into our play clothes, and were eager to open our goodies. All of us sat around filling up our bellies with sweets since it was okay with Mama as long as we ate all of our dinner.

Sunday was definitely the day that our house was filled with the aroma of a family reunion-style dinner. The dining room table was full to capacity with pan fried chicken, baked ham with brown sugar glaze and pineapple rings, potato salad, fresh string beans, stewed corn, "dog bread," rolls, sweet potato pudding, and a pitcher of grape Kool-Aid with slices of lemons and cubes of ice floating on top. Mama also baked a pound cake and sometimes she used country butter to make it, with lemon icing drizzling down the sides. I didn't care for the strong flavor of country butter which I thought had a sour taste. Even though I didn't like the taste of the butter, I still found a way to eat around the edge close to the icing.

Most of the time Bill, Lane, Spring, and I didn't get dessert except on holidays or a special occasion. We did not like to eat green vegetables. Bill hated them worse than the girls. We sometimes gagged while trying to swallow vegetables. Sooner or later, Mama gave in and excused us from the dinner table, although sometimes we had to eat all of it. If we didn't eat all of our food we didn't get dessert; and that was Mama's rule. Many dinners went by when some of us missed out on her delicious cakes and puddings. Sometimes we just couldn't seem to "get down" those green peas, lima beans, and collards. Mama didn't care if you didn't like them, "Eat em' anyway!" she'd say. She worked very hard to help Daddy buy food to put on our table and we were not about to tell her what we didn't like. She was definitely not going to hear that!

Have faith.
It's going to get better.

Learning to Make Do with What You Have

There have been many days that I walked down Merritt Mill Road always keeping in mind memories of my childhood, one being the old house where my brothers, sisters, and I grew up. I recall that the outside was covered with shingles that are now used for covering roofs of a house. Our front door resembled a window with some of the glass panes missing. Plastic sheeting covered the door and all the windows throughout the house to keep us warm during the winter. Our home was heated with two coal burning stoves, one in the living room and one in the dining room, and a wood burning stove in my parents' bedroom. Daddy bought a truckload of coal at a time, that was delivered and dumped in a pile in our back yard. Sometimes when there wasn't enough money to buy a truck load, Daddy drove to the hardware store to buy burlap sacks full and loaded them in the trunk of his car. My siblings and I took turns bringing coal and wood inside for the stoves to keep the house warm. We had to fill buckets from the back yard pile or from the stacks of burlap sacks that were placed at the end of our front porch.

Our hands got extremely black from picking it up, so we decided to make gloves out of paper bags, and sometimes we used newspapers wrapped around our hands. After we made the paper gloves it was easy to clean our hands. We were creative and were always up to something.

The tiny kitchen was where Mama created her recipes. The kitchen was in the back of the house close to the back door. It had a small sink that could only hold a gallon or two of water at a time. Each time after the dishes were washed, there was always water on the floor, but it did not matter because Mama made sure that the floor was swept and mopped every day.

The living and dining room floor was covered with pink patterned linoleum and the rest of the house had hardwood floors. Daddy and Mama laid the linoleum themselves. They purchased the flooring from downtown at the five and dime store in Chapel Hill—it was the cheapest store in town and they were eager to replace the old worn linoleum. The clerk helped my parents carry the long roll and load it in the car. The roll extended from the front seat and hung out of the back window. When Daddy pulled the car up in our driveway, my brothers ran out of the house to help carry the roll of linoleum, and placed it in the middle of the living room floor.

Daddy took a knife that he kept in his pocket, cut open the cardboard tube, and removed the shiny new linoleum. When he unrolled the linoleum onto the floor some of us were instructed to stand on it at the corners so that it would not move or curl up until Daddy and Mama could nail it down. Daddy told Lane, "Stand over there." Then Mama told Spring, "Stand right there." We were all excited and admired the transformation as the rest of us stood around and watched.

Mama is a jack-of-all-trades and there is nothing she will not do or try to do even if she has no idea of how to do it. Daddy knew Mama was going to hang in there with him no matter what it took. We learned a lot by watching her. Daddy was not around the house much, but Mama never missed a beat when it came to raising her children and taking care of her home.

It seemed that when Daddy was home there was always tension between him and Mama. Most of the time they ended up yelling and screaming at each other. I recall one time when Daddy came home mad, usually because he had lost money gambling. He communicated threats to start a fight with Mama. She was ready for whatever he had coming with her arm drawn back with her ice pick for ammunition. When Daddy realized that Mama wasn't backing down, he conceded and left the house. Whenever they fought it really scared all of us kids. Sometimes we cried and cowered behind each other, squatting down with our heads against our knees as if we were praying for relief. After Daddy left the house things calmed down, but Mama sometimes remained angry. It was best to do exactly what she asked or find something quiet to do and stay out of her way. Now when I look back, Mama amazed me how she constantly kept going no matter how tough it got, and there was always work for her to do even when she was at home.

The bathroom was in the back of the house where it was always cold during the winter months. I will never forget the bathtub as it had feet on it. In the summer we took baths in the bathtub. During the winter the three youngest girls took baths one after the other in a big aluminum wash tub. My brothers carried the tub, set it on the newspapers that Mama had spread out in the middle of the floor close to the woodstove in her and

Daddy's bedroom. My sisters and I had to walk back and forth from the bathtub and the kitchen sink faucets filling up pots with warm water, and then pouring the water in the wash tub until it was half full.

Mama was busy preparing the room, and she'd always close the bedroom door to keep the heat inside while we were in the tub. She wedged a piece of folded newspaper between the door jamb and the door knob to secure the door. The same water was used to give the three youngest girls baths. When it was my turn, I stepped into the tub and eased my body into the warm water. I sat down with my knees sticking out so that water would not splash on the floor. Mama scrubbed up and down my body with a bath rag filled with soap. When it was time for me to stand so she could wash my lower body, sometimes the pressure of her strength gave me the feeling that I was going to lose my balance. Often I planted my feet like suctions, gripping the ridges on the bottom of the tub with my toes to keep my balance.

When Mama was done rinsing me off I stepped out onto the newspapers surrounding the tub. She wrapped a towel around me while water dripped onto the newspaper. When I picked my feet up for Mama to dry them print from the old newspapers were clearly visible. You could have probably read the daily news on my soles. I squished and squirmed as my feet tickled while Mama wiped real hard until the print was gone.

The girls' bedroom was in the back of the house also near the bathroom. There was one full-sized bed where the four youngest slept. Two of us slept with our heads at the headboard and the other two at the foot of the bed. In this position we often touched and kicked each other. Whenever we touched each other there was always a fight and we'd yell at each other, "Don't put cha stinkin' feet on me!"

There was also a roll-away bed in the corner of our bedroom where Norma slept. The boys' bedroom was a wide open space that was the entire upstairs shaped like a U with railings all the way around. Going up the staircase was like a grand entrance facing the front door and upstairs. There was a double window facing the front yard. For fun, sometimes my brothers sat outside on the roof to shoot their BB gun and "chunk" rocks.

One night while sitting out on the roof, Yea-Yea was peeking through the leafy branches of the big oak tree in our front yard, and spotted a familiar boy named Bo Pete. Bo Pete was a short fellow and he walked with a limp. One of his legs was longer than the other, and he was constantly teased by other children. Yea-Yea decided to play what he he considered to be a trick on Bo Pete. He went to get Joe and the BB gun that they got for Christmas. After they returned to the window they could see Bo Pete walking across the street near the ice processing plant. They shot their BB gun at the ground near his feet to scare him and to see him run with his bad leg. My brothers quickly jumped back inside the window, hiding while they laughed until they cried when Bo Pete grabbed his leg trying to figure out what the hell was going on. Reminiscing about our childhood acts of terror, I can't believe that we didn't get caught while in the act of doing such mischievous things, especially when Mama would have put a good old fashioned whuppin' on us. For sure, at our house getting a whuppin' was no joke!

The front yard of our house was mostly dirt. We swept it with a broom like it was a floor. We played in our yard most of the time and this is where most of the kids in the neighborhood gathered. Since money was not plentiful at our house in those days, most of the fun and games that we played were created. Whatever games or toys Daddy and Mama purchased we shared with each other, and with the neighborhood children. All of the kids in our neighborhood were Mama's little community.

Jump board was one of our favorite creations. We'd find two or three pieces of old plank board and stack them together on top of two cinder blocks in the middle, similar to a see-saw. One person stood on each end of the board. The object of the game was to see who could jump and land the hardest with our feet to make the person on the other end go as high up into the air as possible.

We jumped high into the air. While gliding we could bend our knees often touching our "butt" to gain strength on the way back down, so that we could stomp our feet hard against the board. When we saw the person on the other end coming down, the person on the opposite end went up into the air. We played jump board until the planks broke and then we walked around the neighborhood to find more.

The girls played hop-scotch almost every day. With a stick in the dirt we drew three blocks; two boxes side-by-side, a single block, and then the two last boxes side-by-side to finish the board. We numbered the boxes from one to eight. Sometimes this process created a cloud of dust. Each of us found a small blunt piece of glass to toss and we hopped on one leg from box to box after tossing our playing pieces, progressing in numerical order until someone reached the box numbered eight. Then we hopped back on the same foot to each box in descending order to win the game. If someone stepped on a line or lost their balance and could not pick up their playing piece they were out of the game.

Today yards are covered with beautiful grass. Now hop-scotch is purchased as a plastic sheeting game or some families buy colored chalk so that their children can draw the diagram on their concrete driveways. Despite the generational change I can still appreciate what my generation learned and accomplished.

My brothers, sisters, and I played a lot of games and were really good at them. The girls always received Jacks for Christmas and in our Easter baskets. We called them "Jack Rocks" because we'd always lose some of them. We replaced the lost ones with tiny rocks that we were able to easily pick up with our hands.

Sometimes we got splinters in our hands from the uneven planks on our front porch where we played jacks most of the time. Mama was not about to let us scratch up her linoleum floor playing Jacks. As long as we didn't lose the ball while playing Jacks, we found something to use to pick up and the game would always go on. Bon was the best player. She tossed them and they'd land all over the floor. Then she tossed the ball high up into the air, while opening her hand, stretching her fingers wide, then scooped up the jacks, and she caught the ball before it bounced one time. The game was over before anyone else got a chance to play. Most of the time we made sure Bon was the last player so each of us could have a chance to play one round.

Whenever my brothers claimed they were bored, they played on the rock piles near the Tin Top neighborhood. It was called this because all of the houses had tin roofs. The gravel pit was where cement was made from sand. There were always giant piles of sand and gravel. My brothers and their friends climbed to the top of the piles and jumped from one to another. If Daddy and Mama had caught them they would have gotten the whuppin' of their lives. This was not only illegal, but dangerous, because the sand and gravel piles could have collapsed and buried them alive. The police had picked up kids before while playing on the rock piles. My parents allowed us to go about our neighborhood as we wanted. We were taught right from wrong and it was up to us to honor our values.

My brothers and their friends rolled car tires for fun and competition. They took them from the junkyard. They brought their tires back to our house, cleaned them to get the white walls spotless. Then all of them began running up and down the streets of our neighborhood to roll their tires. They were very proud of them. Rolling tires was popular and was considered to be a sport in the black community.

The tires were rolled using the fingers and the palm of one hand to go straight, staying in the middle of the tire. To make it go to the right, they touched the tire while it was rolling with the palm of their hand slightly cupped, using a wrist action from underneath; to make it go to the left, they touched the tire the same way with a wrist action over top.

During the last three months of every year there were a lot of exciting events going on. Mama knew she had to take her children out of our neighborhood occasionally to have fun, especially in October for a week every year when it was time for the State Fair in Raleigh, North Carolina. After school let out on Friday of fair week, Mama loaded all of us kids in our red station wagon. The trip to the fair was a reward to us. Daddy bought the used station wagon so that there was enough room for everybody to ride at one time. We had to sit on each other's laps so we could all fit in the car.

Mama drove the car filled with children around the corner in front of my grandparents' house. She pulled up alongside the curb to see if she saw Daddy. "Here he comes!" I yelled, hanging over the front seat of the car. The closer he got to the car the easier I could see this angry look on his face as if, "What the hell do Dip want with me?" I prayed to myself, "Please let him give Mama some money." Otherwise, we could not go and we all were very excited about going to go to the State Fair.

Mama watched Daddy approach the driver's side of the car and he said to Mama, "Dip! What?" She said, "I need money so that I can take the children to the State Fair." Daddy put his hands in his pocket. We all watched when he took a few steps away, turned his back, pulled out a roll of bills, while mumbling as he puckered his lips and gritted his teeth. "They don't need to go anywhere until they learn how to clean up the house." Then he counted money and gave it to Mama. Daddy was never happy about giving up money; that's why his friends nicknamed him "Tight Rope." If the money he was giving up was not going toward the household, Mama had to deal with his attitude to get money for any other reason. I admired her because she always overlooked Daddy's attitude, took the money and we went on our way.

Mama preached to us all the way to the fair about how to conduct ourselves once we entered the fair gates. She also let us know how much money each of us had to spend, so we had better take a good look around before buying tickets for rides or buying food.

I will never forget buying a ticket to see the world's smallest lady. She was housed in a small trailer and everyone inside had to look through a glass window as if she was on showcase. After I got back outside I told the rest of my family what I had seen. They weren't about to waste their money just to look at a lady when they came to the fair to go on the rides. Most of my brothers and sisters decided that they were going to ride the Ferris wheel, and I—with my "scaredy cat" self—

joined in. While I stood in line waiting for the ride to come to a stop, I was as nervous as could be. When I got close to being caged in, I asked the operator if he'd stop if I wanted to get off. He said that he would, but when the Ferris wheel began going around faster and faster, I screamed and yelled for him to stop, but he didn't. When I got off the Ferris wheel I was shaken, and after that incident I never liked riding scary amusement park rides. Afterwards, we walked up and down the midway until everybody was out of money—even Mama.

We left the fair around eleven o'clock that night and all of the kids fell asleep in the car before we got back home. When we arrived home Mama began to holler out our names, one by one, to wake us up.

Thanksgiving time was the next event my family shared, and there was always a feast at our house. All of my immediate family gathered, even my cousin Roy. Mama's sister Myrtle, nicknamed "Big," suffered a fatal heart attack while shopping downtown in Durham when her son, Roy, was just a young boy. Mama raised him just as she had her own children. We considered Roy to be our brother. During the holidays he would come home from college where he was studying to become a teacher.

Daddy was absent, as usual, during Thanksgiving dinner. He always came later after everyone had been served. Nothing stopped or slowed Mama down when it came to preparing her big feast. She had worked all day before coming home on Wednesday evening to start preparing dinner and making cakes. Everybody except Mama sat around eating bologna and cheese sandwiches with potato chips. She was busy creating her dishes. There wasn't much room in the kitchen to cook a meal—let alone a feast. Mama paced from the kitchen to the dining room table where she mixed her cake and pie batters.

I was always happy about Thanksgiving dinner. I knew for sure that on this day I was going to get as much dessert as I wanted, even if I didn't eat all of my dinner. The delicious aroma of grandpa-style fried chicken, roast turkey with dressing and giblet gravy (I love turkey, but I did not like dressing) wafted from the kitchen. Mama also cooked fresh turnip greens, potato salad, candied yams, banana pudding (my favorite), and made sweet iced tea.

I watched as she layered the bananas and wafers and poured on the hot custard. The dining room table was covered with a pink flowered tablecloth, decorated with all our dishes filled with country-style foods and desserts that Mama had created from her recipes, and she kept all of them in her memory. The only space on the table that was visible was the edges where some of the family members ate.

We all gathered around the table and there were only four chairs. Mama told us kids to pull out Daddy's card table from the closet so that we would have more space. We ate wherever we could even if we had to sit on the floor, and that was okay at Thanksgiving for the kids. Mama was always overseeing the dinner to make sure that everyone was fine. Before we ate we all said the Grace together:

God is great.
God is good.
And we thank Him for our food.
By his hands, may we be fed.
Thank You Lord for our daily bread.
Amen

After Thanksgiving Mama used the leftover turkey and prepared turkey pot pie. It looked just like a big cobbler with mixed vegetables with its golden brown crust and the juices bursting through. Leftovers from any big meal were never wasted at our house. Mama preached about the starving kids overseas who would love to have food like ours. The thing that worried me the most about leftovers from Thanksgiving dinner was that the green stuff, and by that I mean some of the vegetables that were not eaten, were going to end up on my plate after all. And of course, once again, some of us missed out on dessert that evening.

Everything got back to normal around our house as the week went by. The stacks of dishes, pots, and pans were finally washed, dried, and put back on the shelves and in the cabinets. Sunday was a real reminder that Thanksgiving was over. Church was definitely going to happen and we returned to school on Monday from our holiday break, but not before my uncle showed up.

Mama's brother, Uncle Jim, was a big, tall man. He was a full-time cook, part-time preacher, and he was full of joy. He laughed and giggled most of the time. He visited a lot, mostly around Christmas or when Daddy was not around. Mama called on him to help keep our attitudes straight. He terrified us kids with his abusive, yet playful nature. He stormed in our house, running to catch us, and pinched whoever he caught. It felt like he had something in his hands, but he didn't.

My brothers spotted his truck as soon as he pulled up in front of our house. They tore the house apart, knocking over chairs or anything that was in their way trying to get out of his sight. Suddenly, the girls began running and crying because we wanted to get away too. I was scared to death, and I thought that Mama was going to let him kill us, but he was only kidding. Uncle Jim sat around our house afterwards and laughed until tears ran down his face. He held his stomach, gasping for breath while he tried to calm down. Coming to our house was an amusement for him that I am sure he looked forward to.

For many years Uncle Jim raised hogs. Some days after he terrorized us he invited my brothers, sisters, and me to come along with him to feed them. We jumped on the back of his truck with the huge tubs of smelly food scraps and rode all the way to the countryside. Riding on the back of his truck was lots of fun. While we were in the city limits we stood up holding onto the handmade wooden extension slats on the sides of the truck bed.

When we reached the countryside we had to sit down as Uncle Jim drove faster. The blowing wind caused us to turn our faces as it took our breath away. Every time he turned a corner the wooden slats creaked like they were going to fall off his truck. Our bodies rocked back and forth, side to side, bumping up and down, and we even bumped into each other, laughing.

After we arrived at his farm, he told us that we could go ahead and feed the hogs. There was a box of baked potatoes that were left over from the fraternity house where he worked. One time, I picked up a potato that was still kind of warm and knocked one of the hogs up side the head. Everybody laughed and did the same thing. We fed the hogs all of the potatoes while Uncle Jim poured the slop in the troughs. The hogs ate everything that was given to them, even the foil on the potatoes. My uncle enjoyed taking us with him. He made sure that he was a part of our lives. After feeding the hogs he drove us to his house for dinner with his wife, Aunt Lula Mae. She was very quiet, reserved, and never had much to say to us. I guess she liked us or she would not have let us spend nights at their house.

During the weeks before Christmas we told Mama what we wanted Santa Claus to bring us. Daddy was not the one to tell, he didn't want to hear anything most of the time, but he knew she needed him to help. As Christmas drew nearer, we cleaned more, and there was no school until after New Year's. Year after year, during the holidays Mama took her kids to meet Santa Claus at the fraternity house on the University of North Carolina campus where she worked. There was a present for every child, but I was scared to death of Santa Claus!

Uncle Jim told my brothers, sisters, and me that Santa was going to put pepper in our eyes if we were bad. I wasn't quite sure what Santa considered bad and my uncle didn't say. Consequently, when I saw that big old white man with a long white beard, I was ready to run for my life. There was no way in the world that I was going to let that big man come near me. I was petrified, sobbing, sniffing with my snotty nose while tears rolled down my cheeks. Mama had to get my present for me. I just stood back in the corner of the room and cried. Sure, I wanted my present, but I also wanted to get the hell out of there as soon as I could.

Our Christmas was not complete without homemade ornaments on our Christmas tree. Mama bought Styrofoam balls, sequins, straight pins, glue, and all kinds of lace to decorate the balls. We were going to have our own Christmas tree decorating party. The day that Daddy and Mama came home dragging our tree through the front door into the living room we all were very excited. Norma began to make popcorn using one of Mama's collard green pots. She poured oil and put a slab of butter in the pot. After that, she poured the popcorn from the hole that she had made at the corner of the plastic bag, and then squeezed the bag with her hand to allow just enough kernels to make a pot full.

Norma grabbed a pie pan from the cabinet to cover the top of the pot so that the popcorn would not pop all over the stove. She held the pie pan with a dish towel while she shook the pot back and forth as the sound of the popcorn repeatedly tapped on the pie pan. It was a very exciting sound to us kids. We knew that there was going to be a lot of popcorn. When the tapping started to die down, the popcorn was ready.

The aroma of fresh popcorn filled the house as Norma poured pot after pot into a large brown paper bag. She had to stop us from eating it so that there was enough to decorate the tree. Mama showed us how to string popcorn, demonstrating how to thread a needle as an example. Once we figured it out we had to thread our own needle until we were finished.

While some of us strung popcorn and cranberries, others made ornaments, and Mama was right there coaching us on. She was creative and for us young children she made the days at our house before Christmas a treat by allowing us to use our own creativity. After all the decorations were on the tree, Mama tossed on the silver icicles. She then sprayed white snow all over the tree. She went from the tree to the windows facing the front of the house to make it look like it had snowed.

Like most parents Daddy and Mama had to hide our Christmas wishes from Santa around the house. Sometimes my sisters and I liked to play hide-and-go-seek in the house. A few days before Christmas, Lane and I found some of our wishes packed away under our parents' bed. I could not believe what we were seeing was real. "Here's our stuff." I said to Lane in a whisper. "Shhhhhh look!" I said as my eyes lit up like a Christmas tree. "Here is our Easy Bake oven and our cotton candy machine." Lane said, "Here's a guitar. Let's get out of here before Daddy and Mama come and catch us in here hiding under their bed. You know if we get caught, we'll get a whuppin'." This was the day that I realized that there was really no such thing as Santa. But I continued to play along for fear that I wouldn't get gifts—as we all know, it comes to an end.

We always received presents for Christmas that we could learn to cook with. Mama felt it was extremely important to teach all of her children to cook, especially the girls. We made real cakes in our Easy Bake oven using the mini prepackaged mixes. When we ran out we used leftovers from Mama's recipes, and poured the batter into the tiny pans that came with the set. We made a table out of an empty box that had previously contained a Christmas gift by turning it upside down on the floor. Mama let us use one of her checkered dish towels for our tablecloth—we prepared our tea set and play dishes to have our own little Christmas dinner.

We sometimes fought over our toys. There was one blue bike for the boys and one red bike for the girls to share, even though I did not know how to ride a bike. I constantly watched my sisters and brothers go up and down the sidewalk, sometimes with no hands, and watching them really made me want to learn. One day, I got on the girls' bike and proceeded down the sidewalk wobbling back and forth while my feet kept touching the ground. I didn't want to fall and scrape my knees, because everyone would know that I had fallen. I used the same path that my brothers and sisters used passing the bumblebee bushes with the lavender flowers. I kept wobbling all the way to the end near the Mason Motel and grocery store owned by a black family who was successful just like my grandparents. I tried very hard to ride our bicycle. I didn't have any luck at first, but one day after dozens of attempts, I finally managed to ride the bicycle. My smile was the size of Chapel Hill on that day, and I was tickled to death. "I got it! I got it!" I yelled proudly so that everybody could hear me, "I can ride a bike now!"

The New Year began with my birthday. Birthdays at our house were a celebration and a time for Mama to show off her hosting talent. With her help, I made a list and invited all the girls in my class. I designed my invitations using colorful construction paper and crayons. I already knew that my birthday party was going to be extra nice, as Mama's specialty was entertaining. The five and dime store downtown was the place she went to shop for colorful plates, napkins, party favors, cups, and a matching tablecloth. She bought candy by the pound from the candy counter to make little bags as party favors for the girls to take home.

The food was always the treat. Mama baked my birthday cake in a sheet cake pan and iced it with butter cream frosting. She nervously placed each piece of the letters that spelled out "Happy Birthday" across the top with letters made from hardened sugar, along with flowers and balloons that came with the decoration pack. She iced the cake the night before—I was right there standing and waiting patiently for the opportunity to lick the spoon and bowl. I scooped out the remaining icing with my long fingers sliding up and down the inside of the bowl eating everything that was left. Sometimes when I licked the bowl, my nose swiped the insides, and I'd run to look in the mirror to laugh at my silly face.

Mama decorated the room by placing colorful bowls of mints, peanuts, potato chips, and popcorn all around the room on different tables. Hot dogs were boiling in a pot and her homemade chili was simmering on the "back eye" of the stove. While the party was going on the ice cream churn was working as hard as my brothers could make it turn. They were busy taking turns operating the churn that was making the "Dip" special recipe for old fashioned vanilla custard. Everyone came to the party dressed really nice, handing me my gift, and taking a seat wherever they wanted in the living room where the linoleum floor was sparkling clean.

My party entertained everyone with games and prizes. Everybody was excited when we played pin the tail on the donkey and bingo and swung at a homemade piñata that Mama and I made using a brown grocery bag from the Colonial store. She doubled the bags and I glued all types of colorful cartoons from the funnies section of the old newspapers that were stacked against the wall for making fires. We filled it with the best of candies that any kid could imagine. Mama hung the piñata in the middle of the door frame between the living and dining room. Each of us kids took a turn to punch at it using a small plastic baseball bat. Mama covered our eyes with a dish towel and fastened it with a safety pin. We all laughed at each other when the towel fell down over our face and covered our nose.

Mama made almost everything and any event that she hosted was always a success. She was so full of love for what she was doing, and most of all, she didn't mind doing anything that she felt was going to make life better for herself and others. Mama wanted always to set an example for her children and the community.

Mama also made time to enjoy her friends. A few of them started "club meetings" around town. Once a month, on a Saturday night, the members traveled to each other's houses as a get-together to discuss different issues and incorporate them with Bible study. My brothers, sisters, and I loved it when it was time for the group club meeting at our house. Mama had her chance to prepare fancy food for them and we knew we would get to sample some of it. She prepared adorable little pimento cheese and chicken salad finger sandwiches. She set out peanuts and mints in lovely glass dishes.

There was always one of her delicious carrot cakes. She used her glass punch bowl to make punch that consisted of Kool-Aid, juice from a can of fruit cocktail with some ginger ale. It was delicious! Mama loved showing off what she knew, and people paid attention to everything she did, especially when she was preparing any kind of food.

The group started every meeting with a prayer. We used to laugh, giggle, and elbow each other as we watched the looks on the ladies' faces. While we were eating the sampling of food that Mama had given us, we peeked through the cracked door from Daddy and Mama's bedroom. As kids we thought their hairdos, shoes, and dresses were hilarious. To top it off, when the group sang hymns, they sang out of tune. It was hard for us to hold back our laughter—we covered our mouths so that we would not make too much noise. We tried to shush each other up from laughing, because if Mama heard us we were definitely in trouble.

The meeting concluded after a second prayer. We knew it was time for us to finish off whatever food was leftover and also to help Mama clean up. Mama never put anybody before her children, and that's why she gave us something to eat while her meeting was going on. While we were finishing the leftovers, we continued to talk and laugh about the personalities of Mama's friends. We knew that the gatherings made her happy. She prepared delicious food and everyone loved it. Therefore, I am sure that cooking and entertaining is truly the essence of my mama.

Be a good listener.
Honor the opinion
of others.

Everything that Happens in Life Is a Learning Experience

I learned from everything that I experienced in my life, whether it was good or bad. I attended daycare at the Holmes Center on Roberson Street in Chapel Hill. Mama and I walked there every morning through the path alongside our house, and over a mud puddle that never seemed to dry up. I jumped over the puddle as I held onto Mama's hand. This path was also the way to my grandparents' house where I hated walking past. I will never forget, Grandma had a tiny Chihuahua that always came running toward us every morning, barking loud at us as if he was going to eat us alive. Grandma came running out the door screaming, "Peeweeeeeee! Peeweeeeeee! Peeweeeeeee! Come back here Peeweeeeeee!" The entire time she called Peewee, yelling his name, he continued to head our way.

I grabbed Mama's arm and ran around her like she was a merry-go-round. When that didn't work, I jumped, grabbing her shoulders wanting her to carry me, because Peewee never listened to Grandma. Mama pushed my arms down, yelling "Get down, that dog ain't gonna bother you!" Grandma continued to yell and she was finally able to grab Peewee. I persisted and tried to jump in Mama's arms, terrified and screaming at the top of my lungs until Peewee was out of my sight.

The only thing that I clearly remember from my daycare experience was that the first thing in the morning every child was given a tablespoon full of cod liver oil, a vitamin supplement. It tasted awful! Afterwards, the teacher gave each child a small plastic cup with orange juice to relieve the bad taste lingering in our mouths. I attended daycare at the Holmes Center until I was six years old and ready for elementary school.

Unfortunately, a few months after I completed daycare I was molested. It was an ordinary day around our house; Daddy and Mama were both working and the rest of the family was outside playing. I ran home while playing at a neighbor's yard to use the bathroom. I realized that I had waited too long when I couldn't stop twisting and turning while hurrying toward the bathroom. Afterwards, I started walking back through the house and noticed that there was a large bumblebee on the screen door. To avoid being stung, I thought if I pushed the screen door open very hard, I could run out fast but I was afraid and started to cry.

I can visualize this scene as if it was yesterday. I noticed a man had come through our back door, a friend of Roy's that I had seen before at our house. When it was not cold our back door was always unlocked as well as the front door during the daytime. The man saw me crying and picked me up as if he was going to console me. He walked swiftly toward the back of the house into the bedroom where my sisters and I slept. He tossed me on the bed quickly as if we were playing a fun game.

He grabbed my shorts by the elastic waist band, pulled them down to my ankles, and pulled me by my legs to the end of the bed. I lay there trying to figure out what on earth was this man going to do to me. I had no idea and he said nothing. I just lay there waiting and stared at him. He proceeded to undo his pants and pulled down the zipper. Suddenly, there was this sound of a door opening. Someone else had come into the house. This man frantically fastened his pants and dashed out the back door. I pulled my pants up while lying on the bed, got up, and went to see who was there. It was a couple of my brothers coming home from selling drinks at the Carolina football game. I never said anything about what had happened to me since I had no idea. I was okay as far as I was concerned, the bumblebee was gone off the screen door, and I ran back outside into the neighborhood to play with my friends.

As I reflect back to 43 years ago, I've thought about this incident about three times. I didn't know at the time what molestation was. When I began writing my manuscript, I realized what it was going to take for me to put my feelings into words. I was consumed with emotions about what really could have happened to me, and how blessed I am to have escaped this potential devastation. My family never knew about my molestation. I later discovered that Norma encountered the same experience by the same man. She was the first family member that I shared my writings with. While I read along she sat and listened to what I was trying to get across to readers. After I finished reading the part about being molested, she knew immediately who the man was. Norma was touched. It brought back her memories and all she could say was, "If Daddy had known he would have killed him."

Daddy went after this man after he had molested Norma. He had no idea that I was also attacked. Today children are taught to be aware of people who touch their bodies inappropriately. When I was coming along as a youngster, I was never told about anything of this nature happening. I now understand the difference in generations, how my upbringing was different from today, and how things have changed. When I was a young girl everybody in the community looked out for each other. At night when it was time for bed, Mama only locked the screen door. Rarely did anybody bother people during these times because of "neighborhood bonding."

Later on in my life, I encountered this man as a customer at our business. He entered the door of the restaurant and I immediately felt this unnerving feeling that I knew him. I noticed him when he greeted Mama and continued to wait for a table with his guest. Once he was seated, I asked Mama, "Who was that man?" She told me, "That's the guy your Daddy was gonna kill because he tried to rape Norma." What Mama said made me remember that this was the man who molested me.

When he walked pass me, my eyes met his, and he had what I thought was an innocent look on his face. I wanted very badly to call the police and have him arrested, but I knew that it was not possible. Norma and I are very grateful that the memories have had no emotional effect on our lives today. We both are also grateful that we survived and had a chance to share our real life "Boogieman" experience.

Years passed and my siblings and I continued to learn about our neighborhood, seeking to have fun—most days in the summer we went to the swimming pool.

My brothers, sisters, and I were curious kids. We sometimes sat on our grandparents' back porch and watched as the

Bynum-Weaver Funeral Home

red ambulance left with its loud screeching sirens and flash-ing lights which indicated that they were going to an emergency scene. If there was a death, the black hearse slowly pulled out of the driveway to bring a body back to the Bynum Weaver Funeral Home.

I jumped out of my chair, opened the screen door, and yelled to whoever was in the house, "Ya'll come here—the hearse brought a dead body!" We watched as the hearse backed up to the rear of the funeral home. A body wrapped in a white sheet was rolled out on a gurney with wheels and the undertakers (morticians) pushed it through the back door to be prepared for viewing.

It seems a bit strange, but my siblings and I learned a lot about our neighborhood by going to the funeral home that was next door to our grandparents' house. Every week meant paying attention to the sign that sat in the front window that verified our curiosity that there was indeed a body for viewing. We were eager to go inside even if we had no idea of who the corpse was. Once we got the nerve, we shoved each other to make someone else go first because some of us were afraid, yet curious to see. Slowly I took steps up to the door, looking behind me to make sure that the family of the deceased wasn't trying to enter. Creepy thoughts ran through my mind when I got closer to entering.

Bon said, "Go ahead, if you're going!" I eased in behind the gang and whispered. "It's dark in here." The lights were dim and a spotlight was shining on the body. I peeked over someone's shoulder to take a glimpse. I wasn't sure if the body was going to move, but I was prepared to run like hell if I had to!

Most of the time there was a dead body prepared for viewing in the parlor room, so that family and visitors could come and pay their final respects. I recall that all of the corpses wore white gloves, and often we discussed where their legs were or if they were wearing shoes. The bottom half of the casket was always closed. After we viewed the body, one after the other signed our names in the guest book.

Before leaving we peeked inside the office to say "Good-bye" to Mr. Bynum Weaver, the funeral director, and ran quickly out the door. He was a tall, thin, dark skinned man. His nose was pointed and he wore large framed black glasses. For a long time we teased each other about his big hands, long fingers and how he always wore a mixed-matched jacket and necktie. The funeral home emergency workers were always on standby, and most of the time during the day Mr. Weaver sat in his big wooden chair in the office waiting for the phone to ring. He often spent the night at the funeral home, falling asleep in his big chair, as that we sometimes noticed when we walked by. At this time, Bynum-Weaver was the only black ambulance and undertaker service in Chapel Hill.

When my siblings and I were not at the funeral home we were always searching for ways to make money. There were many days when we walked around town to find soda bottles to sell at Blackburn's store. When school was out for the summer months we called ourselves "bottle collectors." We collected soda bottles that we found lying around on the ground. Most days we had to find a way to make our own money, because Mama didn't have much to give us, and asking Daddy was out of the question.

We spent hours walking around town in the neighborhoods, through the man-made paths that were created from the many footsteps that traveled through the grounds. People threw their paper, beer, wine, and soda bottles down on the ground as if it was okay. It was okay with us because we made money from trading in the bottles. We looked in ditches, grassy areas of paths, and sometimes crossed the street to look on the other side of the road. We packed our crumpled brown paper grocery bags until they were full or heavy enough that we had to go back home and unload.

At home we rinsed the dirty bottles using the water "spicket" on the side of our house, and organized them neatly by brand before selling them. Mr. Milton, the owner, had already told us after the first time we turned in bottles that he would not accept any more dirty muddy bottles. We made sure that all of our bottles were clean and we stacked them neatly in wooden bottle crates. I used my multiplication skills to calculate bottles to make sure that we were paid for each one we sold.

Community Surrounding My Family

MERRITT MILL ROAD

TIN TOP

SUNSET DRIVE

CRAIG STREET

BYNUM STREET

BROAD STREET

LLOYD STREET

WEST ROSEMARY STREET

WEST FRANKLIN STREET

ROBERSON STREET

GRAHAM STREET

NORTHSIDE

We were paid five cents for the six ounce bottles and ten cents for the sixteen ounce ones. When any one of us found a sixteen ounce bottle, it was like finding money lying on the ground. Everyone knew when I found one because I'd scream and yell with excitement. I don't ever remember leaving the store with leftover money that I made from selling bottles. I made sure that I cashed every cent in for candy, cookies, and a grape Popsicle. I was eager to get back home with my goodies, while I munched along the way. My brothers, sisters, and I walked a long way to find bottles, and besides, I was not about to wait for the next day to satisfy my sweet tooth. Occasionally, my brothers sneaked around to the back of the store to steal empty soda bottles from where they were stacked outside. Then they took them back inside the store as if they had found them and resold them to Mr. Milton. Eventually, he caught on to their game and they were forbidden from selling any more bottles.

At the end of most summers before school began in August, Daddy drove some of us kids and Mama in his Buick Deuce-and-a-quarter to downtown Durham to shop for school clothes. There was not enough room in the car for everyone to go shopping at one time. Durham was a big city to the folks who were from Chapel Hill. Daddy always parked his car near Five Points since this was the major shopping area where five streets intersected. There were many stores and people walking up and down the busy sidewalks, going in and out of the stores. Sometimes the lines in the stores were long and it was hard getting assistance, especially at this time when parents were shopping for school items. I remember Marilyn's shoe store and HS Kress. These were the two stores that were always a part of our shopping trip.

For a long time, the girls' shoes were bought from Marilyn's shoe store except for Bon's. She wore a size eleven when she was twelve years old. Mama shopped at Freeman's because they sold large size shoes and clothes for men and boys. She also bought her shoes at Freeman and she wore a size twelve.

HS Kress was our favorite place to shop because that's where Daddy bought us hot dogs and sodas. They were the best hot dogs we had ever eaten that weren't made by Mama. Sometimes he bought us popcorn and Mama got hot roasted peanuts and everything was ordered to go. We ate in the car on the way back home; sometimes we sat in the car while in the parking lot downtown, and ate our food while Mama finished shopping for the boys.

An entire day was used to shop for eight children. Joe never went shopping. He stayed at home to hang out with his friends. When we retuned home he never liked the clothes Mama had picked out for him to wear. I could never understand why he didn't want to come along and get new clothes. I was always happy when he wanted to stay at home because that meant there was more room for me in the car. There was never a problem to get the girls to go shopping. The thought of leaving us behind was out of the question. We didn't care if we had to sit in the hot car as long as we were able to go. I guess my brother was smart about refusing to come to shop. He did not enjoy hanging around when Mama was not shopping for him.

In downtown Durham, regardless of the business of downtown, I was aware of the somewhat sweet yet unpleasant odor of processed tobacco. It was noticeable at Five Points and became even more prominent as we neared the Liggett & Myers Factory. I was also unaware of the political climate at that time. Due to the type of labor needed, Liggett hired more blacks than any other company in the city. North Carolina Mutual, Mutual Savings & Loan and Mechanics & Farmers Bank on Parrish Street were black-owned. Only the Spaulding family, the owners, and their close friends were working in these businesses. It was sarcastically referred to as the "Black Wall Street." Duke Hospital only hired blacks as housekeepers to work in the hot and sweaty laundry.

I learned later in life that we ate our hot dogs and popcorn in the car because blacks were not allowed to eat in the inner city restaurants. There were black and white designated water fountains even in the stores where blacks were allowed to shop. At that time, I never noticed that blacks and whites even walked on different sides of Main Street.

How could someone my age sense the sweltering acts of racism and the ugliness of segregation, which set Durham apart from smaller towns like Chapel Hill. I know now that Daddy and Mama knew what it was like, but they never attempted to explain it to us. After all, why invade our innocent minds with something we wouldn't understand?

Later on, I was made aware of what happened during this time among blacks in Durham, and the growing unrest of segregation throughout North Carolina that made newspaper headlines. Yes, later on, I learned of the clashes between whites and blacks. I learned of blacks sitting in the normally white seats at restaurants until they were arrested. I watched on TV and learned of the fire bombings, race riots, and the visits throughout the country from the late Dr. Martin Luther King Jr. But through it all, I remember Durham as a shopping haven for our family where we were together and had fun.

One time after we got back home from shopping, I rushed inside to put my new clothes in the closet so that I could go outside to play in the neighborhood. It seemed like I had just gotten outside when Mama stuck her head out the screen door and called me from down the street where I was playing. She yelled my name really loud, "Neeeeeecy!" When I heard Mama screaming my name it startled me, and I thought that I was in trouble. I ran as fast as I could to see what she wanted. She told me, "Go to Colonial Store and buy two boxes of washing powder—the one that cost two for forty-nine cents. Take this dollar and come right back!"

The store was around the corner and across Franklin Street. Since I did not want to go alone, I asked Brenda our next door neighbor's granddaughter to come with me. I was glad that I had asked her to come with me—she was lots of fun. Brenda was my best friend and was always the girl who played around our yard. She and I created imitation meals using mud. We scooped up loose dirt with our hands and used water from the outside "spicket." We mixed our recipes in an old plastic cup or can that we found lying around our neighborhood. Sometimes we invited other girls from our neighborhood to join us to imagine that we were a family.

Brenda and I skipped most of the way to the store, until we had to stop for a moment to catch our breath and empty the dirt out of our shoes. We both entered the store, passing the grocery carts, while I went directly toward the household cleaning section of the store. Brenda went in the opposite direction. I found what Mama sent me to buy, and I headed to the register to check out.

I knew that Mama was waiting for me to return home and I was in a hurry to go straight back to avoid punishment. After I finished paying for the washing powder at the register I did not see Brenda. "Where is she?" I thought. I went back around through the front entrance to find out where she was. I looked down every aisle until I found her down by the candy. I saw her talking with a man who looked like he worked in the store. When I got closer to them I noticed that something was wrong.

Brenda had an innocent look on her face and I found out that she had stolen a bag of candy. The bag had been found punched open by the store clerk with pieces of candy missing. When the clerk saw me walking up, he automatically assumed that I was involved. I was terrified and I knew what Mama's reaction was going to be when she found out. I knew that I was in trouble. I never imagined that Brenda would do something like this. She had never gotten into this kind of trouble before.

The store clerk called our parents' from the office to inform them of what had allegedly happened. After he made the phone calls, he sent us on our way, and we headed toward home. I never thought that I could walk so slow in my life. My heart raced and I was frightened to face Mama, even though I was innocent of any wrongdoing. When Brenda got home, her uncle was waiting for her on the front porch of their house. I could hear her screaming and crying from the whuppin' that she was getting and when her grandmother got home she was whupped again.

Well, I got my whuppin' also for inviting Brenda to come along. When I finally stepped my feet inside our house, I noticed that Mama was shaving the leaves off a switch that she had pulled off the bush from the yard. It had about six stems sticking out that she intertwined to make it durable. When she began to swing the switch at me it seemed like I was tap dancing, jumping around on the floor hoping to get at least one leg out of the way so that she would not hit it. It did not matter, I could not run, so I just hung in there until she was done. I will never forget that day, and I've learned that sometimes you are found guilty and punished merely by the company you keep.

Segregation still existed when I attended grade school at one of the two black schools in Chapel Hill in the early sixties. Northside Elementary School is where black students attended from first through the sixth grade. Seventh through twelfth grade students attended Lincoln High School.

Before we could start elementary school we had to receive inoculations. Mama had to bring our immunization records to the school to verify that we were up-to-date. When it was my turn she took me to the health department—we stood in line and waited until my name was called to get my "shot." I held onto Mama's hand tightly while tears ran down my face. I dreaded getting "shots," easing along behind Mama hanging onto her skirt. I was instructed to sit down in a chair as the nurse sterilized by arm with a cotton swab while Mama stood next to me. I screamed as loud as I could when I felt that stinging pinch. The process was over quick and a bandage was placed on my arm. Mama caught hell, especially when it was time for one of her children to go to the doctor. Year after year she had to deal with us as we constantly pitched fits of terror.

Northside School was located at the dead end on McMaster Street. The school buses dropped off the students who lived in the countryside where the roads were muddy red clay when it rained. Students who lived in town had to walk to school. The walk was a relatively long way and it seemed even longer in the winter.

One day, I remember one kid who was having a severe asthma attack was standing at the top of the hill gasping for breath in the freezing cold. I asked him, "Are you ok?" He nodded, and said "Uh-huh," while trying to gain his composure. By this time, my brothers, sisters, and I found a short cut to school. We had to walk from Merritt Mill Road down Roberson Street, passing Hargrave recreation center, then through the woods and down a steep hill where a creek ran at the bottom. Kids crossed the creek or walked all the way around through town, which made the journey much longer than the time we needed to get to school.

The hill that we had to go down was very steep. Some days I held onto other kids to keep from falling, and sometimes I squatted down on my "butt," so I could keep my balance. I watched other kids who took the same path, following their techniques, and my books still fell out of my arms and down the rocky hill. I'd grab branches that were sticking out of the ground to ease myself down the hill.

When I got to the bottom I gathered my books, brushed myself off, and prepared to cross the creek.

The key to crossing the creek was to take steps carefully on the fallen trees that were lying across it, and to step onto the rocks that were sticking out of the water. If we lost our balance we stumbled in and our feet got wet. By watching Mama, I was always observant, constantly paying attention to others' mistakes and successes, and learning from them. Sometimes we made it across the creek without falling and sometimes we got wet. Either way, it wasn't fun to have wet feet in the middle of the winter and have to walk around all day with soggy feet.

Often we got briars stuck in our hands and fingers from the bushes on the hill. After we got across the creek, we had to climb yet another steep, bushy hill, and finally we made it to school. However, in the winter our feet and hands were throbbing and felt like they were frozen.

There wasn't a cafeteria at Northside for a few months because of renovations. The lunches were brought in by the dairy trucks. My brothers, sisters, and I were not allowed to eat from the free lunch program. Daddy did not permit his kids to be part of any program that insinuated that he could not provide for his family. While his pride was in our way, we missed out on some good school lunches that we really wanted very badly.

Mama usually packed peanut butter and jelly sandwiches for us with some saltine crackers and a couple of cookies in our lunch bag. One day I remember opening my lunch bag—I pulled out a peanut butter biscuit wrapped in wax paper and after I opened the crimpled wax paper, my head began to sag with a grim look of disappointment on my face.

Mama forgot to put jelly on my sandwich. I did not like the idea that I had to eat peanut butter on a biscuit. The dough inside a biscuit when it is cold made swallowing more difficult for me, not to mention adding peanut butter to it. During my childhood, choices were not available—we took what was given to us even if we weren't always happy with it.

After school the rule was to take off our school clothes and put on old worn clothes. The newer clothes were saved as much as possible so that they would last longer before we grew out of them. The next time any clothes were bought was in June for the summer months. We were not about to go outside and play kickball in our good clothes that Daddy and Mama bought for school and church.

When my brothers, sisters, and I changed out of our school clothes, homework was the first thing on our agenda. After our homework was done we played outside. We used the trees, bushes in the yard, and parts of the porch as bases to play kickball. Most days while we played outside, Norma was in the kitchen warming our dinner that Mama had previously prepared and left on the stove. On Friday evenings, Norma toasted bologna and cheese sandwiches for all eight of us for dinner if Mama didn't have a chance to cook before she went to work.

We always had to be in the house before dark. Dinner was served around seven o'clock—just about the time Mama was getting home from her third job as a maid. Daddy worked and hustled to make extra money while Mama was a workaholic. My parents without a doubt took good care of their children, and Mama did it with every breath that she had. I never heard her complain about being tired or talk about taking a day off.

Even when Mama was not working she brought home clothes to iron to make extra money. Sometimes when I opened the refrigerator, I found shirts that she had starched because she wanted them ironed to a crisp. Norma helped Mama iron clothes and she also helped out a lot around the house cleaning. The rest of the family considered Norma as Mama's backup.

Daddy was back up when it came to money. Being the only child, he wasn't used to so many of us trying to get him to do chores around our house. Hustling was his second and third job. He was taught to work hard as he shadowed his parents who also worked hard in their restaurant business. Daddy believed that men should do what ever it takes to care of their family—even if they have to hustle.

Try something new. Make what you have better.

Bill's BBQ, Our Road Map to Entrepreneurship

William Minor, my grandfather, was a light-skinned, short man with curly hair. He slicked his hair down on his scalp with Pomade to swing as many hairs as he could over his bald spot. He was a calm and friendly man who made a living working seven days a week. He was called the "Merchant Man" by the blacks in our town and his grandchildren called him Grandpa. He built his own successful restaurant a few steps out of his back door called Bill's BBQ. He operated and managed the restaurant, and cooked a lot of the food. Most of his menu consisted of prepared items that did not require a lot of ingredients to make. He created his own BBQ sauce, hushpuppies, cole slaw, giblets and noodles, and hot dog chili. Fried chicken and BBQ were his specialty and that's what he made most of his money selling.

Grandpa's restaurant was a fast-food type sandwich eatery with a few boxed meals. The name Bill's BBQ was painted on the front window with white letters and outlined with red paint. He also painted it on both sides of his delivery van along with the telephone number. Inside the restaurant the menu hung on the wall behind the steam table near the cash register. Items on the menu were spelled out by using peg-like letters that were inserted in grooves of the plastic menu board given to him with a drink box from Coca-Cola Bottling Company. Most of his complete lunch and dinner meals included French fries, lettuce with a slice of tomato topped with a dab of mayonnaise, and hushpuppies. The university allowed Grandpa to park his van at the front gate where game goers could purchase boxed meals before entering the stadium. Thousands of boxed fried chicken meals were sold at UNC football games.

Grandpa overworked himself and he always took BC powders throughout the day with a six ounce bottle of Coke. I didn't know if he was in pain, tired, or if he was addicted to taking it. I often watched him because he was in the same spot when he swallowed a pack of BC's on his back porch, where my siblings and I hung out. Most of the time he wore greasy stained pants with his white apron hanging to the side. His front pockets always bulged with his wallet, crumpled receipts, coins, and the bundle of keys on his keychain. Grandpa was everywhere he was needed. I watched him many days as he checked on the pork shoulders cooking in the steaming BBQ pit. He fried tons of chicken, then he acted as a chauffeur for his workers, picking them up and taking them home. Then he called it a day.

When Grandpa first opened Bill's BBQ, Daddy worked there after he finished his primary job. Grandpa taught him how to cut whole chickens into parts, and on occasion, Daddy cut up chicken all day long. My brothers watched as he shoved his hand inside the chicken to remove the small sacks that contained gizzards, necks, and livers, and toss them in the nearby sink. Then they picked up the sacks, tore

Bill's BBQ original delivery menu

them apart, separated the pieces, stuffed them into smaller plastic bags, and sealed them with a twist tie. Daddy sold the chicken parts to make extra money.

Some Saturdays, Daddy drove with my brothers throughout the black neighborhoods in Chapel Hill and Carrboro selling chicken parts packed in a cooler full of ice in the trunk of his car. The bags of chicken parts sold for fifty cents per bag, and often he gave bags to people who could not afford them. Daddy was a tough man with a kind heart. There was always some kind of hustle for him to make extra money for his family. My brothers, sisters, and I made sure we were around to laugh, while we watched him smile, making a blowing sound with his mouth as if he was cooling the dollar bills off while he counted his money. My brothers also learned how to cut chickens as they were right by Daddy's side during the summer, preparing to work when they were old enough.

Grandpa started the first food delivery service restaurant business in Chapel Hill. That's when Yea-Yea began working as one of the delivery boys. Joe took on the task of learning to fry chicken and Norma helped work the counter as a short order cook. The delivery business was a large part of the restaurant's sales, and Grandpa also used Daddy's station wagon. The cars were packed with boxed dinners that many of the college students loved.

"Move out of the way!" Daddy said to me as I always stood around to check out the busy scene while the delivery workers were loading up cars. Sometimes they had to use their personal cars. The rest of my siblings were too young to work inside the restaurant at the time and it didn't take Grandpa long to figure out something for each of us to do. He showed us how we could make money by folding boxes that he used to pack the restaurant's dinners. We made the boxes in the back of the restaurant in a storage room that housed two long tables that he built. The tables were wobbly, but it didn't take much to hold the boxes that were stacked to the ceiling. We made 100 boxes each and were paid a penny for each one. Grandpa used a lot of boxes and we called them "chicken boxes," because that's what he sold the most of.

We taught ourselves how to make the boxes faster by folding five boxes at a time, taking them apart, inserting the four tabs, and closing the flap. We had to make sure that the creases were folded well; Grandpa didn't like it when the boxes wouldn't stay shut. After we finished making chicken boxes, he reached down in his bulged pocket, jingling coins as he pulled out a handful. He paid us and we were happy with our four quarters for a job well done. We had enough money for swimming, movies, Blackburn's store, and sometimes we had to use some of our money to put in Sunday school.

My brothers, sisters, and I were not the only ones that liked to hang out at the funeral home. When Grandpa was not at home he sat on the wooden bench under the big oak tree in front of the funeral home along with the rest of the old men who were retired. They came every day around noon, sat there most of the day, and talked about old times. They stared at people when they walked by and sometimes when I passed by them they stared at me. One day I said to one of the men sitting on the bench, "What cha lookin' at old man?" He replied, "You just keep on livin', you'll get old one day." At my young age I was well aware of the point that he was trying to get across to me. I never forgot his response because he made sure that I understood what it mean to be alive, even if it meant being old. "Well," I said to myself as I walked away, "I want to live, and I guess I will get old one day." Even though I knew what he meant, I quickly put it out of my mind because it was time to play. Wuuuuupeeeeeee!

Mary Minor, my grandmother, was a frail woman with gray hair. She never went without her wig that she used to cover the bald spot on the top of her head. Folks around town called her "Miss Mary." My brothers, sisters, and I called her Grandma. This was the woman whose name I was called as a nickname when I was growing up. Most of the folks around town thought my facial features resembled hers. Grandma had big lips and her lower lip hung down to her chin. I never liked being called "Mary Minor," I liked my own name. I thought our only resemblance was our light-colored eyes.

I was shy when I was called by her name. I knew that I looked a little like her. My brothers and sisters called me "big lips" when we were growing up to make fun of me. My lips were in no way the size of Grandma's—they were just being mean. I loved my grandma; she was a kind woman to our family and everyone she knew around town. Grandma was well-known around Chapel Hill in both black and white communities. Before Grandpa built Bill's BBQ she worked for white folks cooking and cleaning. At the restaurant she assisted him with hiring and training their staff. She was the baker and made all of the desserts for the restaurant.

Grandma taught all of her grandchildren how to make sweet potato pie batter and to roll pie crust. My older brothers and sisters were the first ones in my family to help her. When Lane, Spring, and I were old enough, Grandma taught us how to make her pie recipes, and we were all very happy to learn. On Sunday evenings around seven o'clock we'd walk as fast as we could past the back door of the funeral home and over to Grandma's to help her make sweet potato pie.

After we got inside the house there was an antique hand mirror that hung on the wall next to the refrigerator. When Grandma asked us to get eggs we had to pass the mirror and we'd jump to see our faces. I used to think that we would never grow tall enough to see in the mirror. Upon returning with the eggs, we took turns mashing the chunks of cooked sweet potatoes that Grandma put in a large aluminum bowl. We had to break a lot of eggs into a smaller bowl and beat them with a wire whisk. Then Grandma added the sugar and poured in the melted butter for us because the pot was hot. Afterwards, she dumped in the spices and poured in the milk as we stirred. She then poured the batter into a large bucket and put it in the refrigerator until the next day.

After we finished making the batter for the pies, Grandma paid each of us with a Kennedy coin that she retrieved from her handkerchief that was tied tight and kept in her bosom. Then she stood on her back porch and watched us run home. My sisters and I screamed when we passed the funeral home at night, running with excitement to hurry and get home.

Grandma baked the biggest sweet potato pies that we had ever seen. They were cut into huge slices and sold in the restaurant along with her delicious apple pies. If we were at her house the day she was baking pies we watched her take them out of the oven with her bare hands while they were piping hot. She held onto the edges very lightly with the sides of her hands facing up, and in a flash she placed them on the counter to cool. Her hands seemed tough, and she told us that she had been using this procedure for years. While Grandma was taking the pies out of the oven all we could do was stare with amazement. She never got burned. Afterwards, each of us indulged in a slice of her golden brown deep-dish sweet potato pie while it was still warm. Even today, I can still imagine the taste of nutmeg, sugar, and butter with each bite. We were thrilled that we were paid for helping her make pies.

My grandparents were glad that they had eight grandchildren. We were all eager to assist them in any way they would let us and they always paid us for any work we did for them. Mama sometimes thought my grandparents spoiled us. They also never told us no and gave us whatever we asked for. We could order any food we wanted from Bill's BBQ.

Once a month on a Saturday, Lane, Spring or I walked with Grandma to the Thrift shop to help her pick out stockings. Most of the stockings were donated from Belk's downtown Chapel Hill along with many other items they were unable to sell. I remember the trip down the sidewalk, passing the funeral home and the Laundromat.

"Come on, Grandma!" I said. She walked very slowly and dreaded crossing the street. I waited at the curb until she caught up with me and I grabbed her hand while we crossed Graham Street. After we got inside the store Grandma went directly to the bin that was filled with all sorts of stockings, socks, and handkerchiefs. While she was digging through the bin to find stockings, I was checking out the old pocketbooks—I collected them. I opened each one to look inside at the name of the designer and to see if I saw New York—then I knew it was an expensive handbag when it was originally purchased. When we were not going with Grandma to the Thrift shop we taught her how to read.

Grandma also paid us for teaching her how to read her favorite book, The Bible. For me, teaching grandma to read was a spiritual affair. I was in the seventh grade and I had never opened the Bible away from church until the day I began to teach her. The verses that I taught her to read were also my introduction to the Scriptures in the Bible. I did not understand everything that I taught Grandma to read; she never explained, and I never asked. But I knew that I was making a difference in her life when she began to remember words. She told me, "I didn't finish the third grade. I had to work and help provide for my family."

When I reflect on my life compared to my grandma's, it amazes me how determined she was to read in spite of her lack of education. When it was my turn to help her, I opened the big white Bible, laid it across her lap while we sat on her wrought iron bench on their front porch, and she began to read.

The view was her beautiful rose garden. Grandma said, "The...Lord...is...my...." I said, "shepherd." Grandma repeated, "shepherd." She continued to say, "I..." Then I would say, "shall." Grandma repeated "shall" and she paused again. I said, "not want." Grandma said, "not want." We constantly read to Grandma as her progression took time and was worth every second spent.

Grandma attended church for every occasion that was acknowledged. She was a member of St. Paul's. She went to church, prayer meeting, Sunday school, anniversaries, and usher board meetings.

Sometimes she invited Reverend and Mrs. Duhart over for dinner on Saturday evenings. She pulled out her finest china, sterling silver, and crystal glasses. I remember watching her set the table with her fine linen tablecloth and making coffee using her sterling silver tray set. A table was set for two and Grandma served them as if they were royalty. Grandma loved St. Paul's church and she also loved Reverend and Mrs. Duhart—they were very special to her.

Build your dream.
Let the legacy
continue.

Young Merchants, Surviving the Integration Experience

N orth side Elementary and Lincoln High, the only black schools, were closed. Chapel Hill High School, then located on Franklin Street downtown, where white students attended, was also closed. A new high school was built for both black and white students to attend. Hence, the Chapel Hill public school system was now integrated. This was the beginning of our integration experience.

My brothers, sisters, and I did not pay much attention when integration was announced on TV and discussed among the black community, until the day it became a reality. We were not prepared for what it was going to be like. Mama told me that I was assigned to Estes Hills Elementary School to attend the sixth grade along with Spring. Weird thoughts went through my mind. "What am I suppose to say to 'em?" I didn't know whether or not I would be liked by the white children. The thought of going to school with white students seemed a bit scary for me, but I managed a little better than some of my other family members.

Lincoln High School, Chapel Hill Schools

The day finally came when students who lived in the city limits were allowed to ride the school bus. On the first day of school I wasn't sure how I should feel about what the day was going to be like. I got off the school bus and entered the lobby near the office. I was told by a white lady wearing glasses, hugging a clip board that I should walk around to the classrooms and to find out who my teacher was going to be from the list of alphabetized names on the doors. When I found the door that had my name on it, I looked twice at the other names to see if I knew anyone else who was in my class that came from Northside. There were a few of my old schoolmates' names that I remembered from Northside along with my teacher, Mrs. McDougle. This was a different situation for me being in an environment with white children. With my hands cupped over my eyebrows, I took a peek inside the small glass on the door of the classroom to see how things looked before I went inside. The class was half full of seated students. I opened the door, walked to the back of the classroom, and took a seat while looking straight ahead. I shyly looked out of the corner of my eyes to take a glimpse very slowly at the other students hoping no one noticed me.

My class waited for the other students to find their seats before the late bell rang. The teacher walked in the classroom and I smiled when I saw her. By this time I was happy to see someone I knew who had taught me in third grade. Mrs. McDougle was again going to be my teacher at a time when I felt alone. I was very relieved, took a deep breath, and exhaled with total happiness. I knew that she wasn't sure about what the day was going to be like either. I was certain that it was definitely a change for both of us. Mrs. McDougle made my life easier by being there as a black woman from a black environment.

At this time in my life, I did not realize how few blacks there were until we got around white people. I had been around mostly blacks for so long that I never even thought of being in the same room where they were the majority. I found out that some of the myths about white people were not true. I was happy to find out that a lot of the white students were friendlier than I expected. I wasn't about to discuss integration with anyone—I just wanted my first year experiencing integration to be all right. Recess was the time to meet friends and that's where I met several new students. I was no longer afraid of being around white students. They were in no way a physical threat to me. I survived and my experience educated me in the areas of race relations that I did not know. Sixth grade turned out to be a good year. Before I knew it sixth grade was over, and the next stage began. During my seventh grade year at Guy B. Phillips Jr. High, my brothers, sisters, and I made our debut as merchants.

"Wake up!" Mama screamed at the top of her voice, "Wake up!" Every morning the same phrase echoed throughout our house and it seemed like her voice was bouncing from wall to wall. "Bon, William, Neecy, Spring, Lane, Yea-

Yea, Joe Nathan!"—one after the other. "Get up!" she yelled again, "Ya'll better not miss that school bus. Norma Frances, get up and I mean right now!" Again and again Mama screamed at us until she knew all of our feet were on the floor. We all jumped to our feet as the tone of her voice scared the "livin'" daylights out of us, and she didn't even have to leave her bedroom.

The kids in our neighborhood had to catch the school bus at the top of Church Street, two blocks up the street from where we lived. The bus was always full when it left our bus stop. Some mornings we were late and the bus would already be at the bus stop loading kids. We yelled to the kids boarding the bus, "Hey, tell the bus driver to wait for us!" We ran as fast as our legs and feet could go. When the bus driver saw us he stopped and we began gasping for breath while we continued to run. After I got both of my feet inside the bus I stopped for a moment to catch my breath. By this time I knew that there wasn't going to be any seats left. I stood in the middle of the bus isle holding on to the back of seats. I finally thought that I had calmed down, when the bus driver turned a curve and I fell over onto the seats where students were sitting. I couldn't wait to get off the bus. Missing the bus was not good because Daddy and Mama had already gone to work and the walk to school was about three miles. However, missing the school bus was not as bad as missing a day of school, especially if our parents found out. We went to school even if we had to walk.

Most of the time we got up early so that we would have enough time to stop at the store and buy candy to sell to the students before school began. We took the short-cut through a path behind the old Northside School building that closed after integration. In our community there was an old house used for a store. There wasn't a sign outside indicating that it was a store, but everyone in the surrounding neighborhoods knew the owner, Mr. Bynum Weaver, who also operated the funeral home. The siding was made from shingles decorated with old soda bottle top advertisements. Two creaky, rotten plank board steps got us inside, while we held onto the doorknob as it screeched when we pushed it open. Mr. Weaver repeated several times, "C'mon in, Mizzzzzzes Joe-Diddy." He called my brothers, sisters, and me the combination of both our parent's names. It seemed that this was going to be a life time announcement when he saw one of us. People around town always called us, "Dip Youngins."

Everything in the store was behind a glass case. If customers wanted anything they had to point and ask him for it. No one was about to touch or grab his candy. I pressed my finger against the glass case pointing to the items that I wanted. The case was about five feet long sitting on a wooden frame. Inside the case, boxes of goodies were stacked on top of one another, making it difficult for him to retrieve exactly what I wanted. Then I had to help him find my items. I repeatedly said, "Over here, no, not that, yes, that's it." Some days it took much longer than others as he tried to figure out what his school-age customers wanted to buy, and occasionally he made us late for the bus. He was the only person who worked at his store; if he didn't have time to open the store, it was closed. Mr. Weaver hustled back and forth from the store to the funeral home.

There were shelves across the back wall of the store above his head that held the large clear buckets of Ginger Snaps, Coconut Macaroons, and butter cookies (my favorite). I loved to buy them because they were two for a penny just like the ones I had purchased back at Blackburn's Store when my family lived on Merritt Mill Road. It did not take much money to buy a bag full of anything you wanted there.

We used our lunch money as our bank to buy candy to sell for a profit. I remember buying a whole box of sweet and sour pops. They were sour apple green on one side and had a sweet frosty white coating on the other side. I always bought a box of Rocky Road ginger bread plank cookies. The rest of my brothers and sisters bought their candy and we jumped out the door of the store because we heard someone screaming, "The bus, the bus!" We all started to run as fast as we could so that we would not miss the bus. Here we go again, hoping that the bus driver saw us through the rear view mirror, yelling and screaming, "Wait for us, hey, wait for us!" Many days we had to run and catch the bus.

None of us could touch Bon with a ten-foot pole when it came to selling her items. Not only was she the best one of us at playing Jacks, she was also a true sales-person. Bon made huge candy apples and rice crispy treats at home. She was constantly sought after by students wanting to buy her homemade goodies. She was not going to let any one of us outsell her. Bon made sure that customers could identify her from the rest of us. She stood out in the crowd as she held her candy apples wrapped in buttered wax paper high above her head. She also held onto a large brown paper sack in the other hand loaded with more goodies. Once a week she went down to Village Pharmacy drugstore after school to buy cinnamon oil and a box of toothpicks. She soaked the toothpicks in the oil to make cinnamon toothpicks and sold them too. Cinnamon toothpicks became very popular among students at school. Therefore, I decided to join in and sell them also. I knew there were more students than she could supply. Students were walking around school with a toothpick stick-

Bon frying chicken

ing out of their mouths and some were so spicy that the students sometimes held them.

When the bus arrived at school most of the white kids knew that we were merchants selling some of the best candy that they could buy at any store. We had black customers, too. As we began walking toward the double doors to the school's side entrance, everyone began to gather around us creating a huge scene. We told them that they should start a line, but nobody listened because they wanted to buy our goodies and hurry on to class. We sold as much as we could before the bell rang for class to start and then again at recess. By the end of the day the only thing left in our hands was our lunch money in addition to the profits that we collected that day.

We made many of our classmates happy, especially the white kids because some of them told us that their parents wouldn't allow them to have candy, so this was a treat for them. When the school administration found out that we were "making a killing'" they asked us to stop. The hallways flooded when students saw us coming, but we had to stop. It was okay because we found another way to make money.

A few months later the school decided to open a store on school grounds called the Snack Shack. It was near the bus parking lot where students could buy junk food before and after school. I couldn't believe they stole our idea. We watched Daddy hustle to make money so naturally we were eager to hustle too. Even though we were merchants, students still faced racial issues.

Norma was in twelfth grade at Chapel Hill High School when black students became hostile when the rights of black citizens were being violated. It was a struggle for Chapel Hill black students to deal with how they were being treated nationally. None of "Dip's" children were taught to be violent, but I guess you could see it coming. One evening as we were watching the news, we viewed how black men, women, and even children in Alabama were being clubbed by police. They were bitten by German shepherd dogs and knocked down with high pressure water hoses by firemen. It was truly gut-wrenching to see how these people were being treated merely for marching for their God-given rights. I could see the anger on Joe's face as his eyes appeared to tear up. I noticed the tenseness in his body as he clenched and unclenched his fists. I had never seen Joe disturbed like this about anything before. What happened the next day impacted his life forever and now we realized "real racism."

Joe watched as a white male student slapped a black teacher. Then a riot broke out. The student was trying to stop a fight, but Joe did not feel that the student should have gotten involved. The black students at Chapel Hill High School staged sit-ins. By the time I arrived at Chapel Hill High School in tenth grade, I remember violence erupting.

On another occasion a black student was treated so unfair that it was time to speak out against the injustice. After this happened black students continued to stage sit-ins and block the doors at school. At this time, Joe, along with other black students, started fighting white students, mostly out of anger for the rights of blacks in America. That's why Joe and others were intolerant of this kind of unfair treatment among people of color.

Most black students demonstrated their feelings. Students who didn't want to get involved stayed at home those days. The fights did not last long, but they became frequent, and the principal had to call in the police to help calm things down. One day when a group of students were taunting each other in the commons area, Joe picked up a desk from a classroom, tossed it into the crowd, and hit a student. The actions of my brother caused the principal to send him home that day telling him that he was expelled from Chapel Hill High.

The school called Daddy and Mama and told them what had happened. Mama went to the school with her hands on her hips to find out exactly what her son had done that caused him to get kicked out of school. She wanted to know what she could do to get Joe back in school. This was no joke for my parents. Their goal was to make sure that all of their children graduated from high school and Joe was no exception.

Joe knew that he was not allowed to fight at school.

Leaving school didn't seem to bother Joe at the time, but it bothered Daddy and Mama. The rest of the family didn't like the idea that the school wasn't going to give our brother a second chance. Daddy decided that Joe needed a change of lifestyle and sent him down to Swan Quarter along the coast of North Carolina to live with Roy, who was teaching high school. Joe moved to Swan Quarter to finish high school, but hung out with the wrong crowd and got into trouble. Joe came back home after about three weeks.

I distinctly remember Swan Quarter was a swampy town which bred mosquitoes. We often drove down to visit Roy and his family during the summer. However, we never went outside unless we were going to get in our car and drive someplace. Those darn mosquitoes were waiting to penetrate our skin and suck our blood from the first thing in the morning to the last thing at night. The mosquitoes even found their way through our clothes. I was happy when we returned to Chapel Hill.

When Joe came back home there was nothing much that he could do, and Daddy decided that maybe he'd call his best friend, Jim, who lived in Louisville, Kentucky to see if Joe could try to make something out of his life there. Jim decided that it was okay for my brother to move there, as he was happy to be able to make a difference. Perhaps he could help Joe get a job where he had worked for many years at the cigarette manufacturing company. Joe moved to Louisville and got a job at the same company where Jim worked. Daddy and Mama were very happy that Joe was finally at a place in his life where he could continue to mature and become a responsible, productive citizen.

It was important to my parents to make sure that all their children were productive citizens. This meant not just having a job, but also making decisions based on good judgment. Employment was necessary as it helped to build our character and also gave us a sense of responsibility and accomplishment.

Educate yourself.
It's the key
to learning.

Building
a Community
around Mama

The time came when Daddy and Mama were making enough money for our family to move into a nicer house. Daddy had opened a pool hall that was doing well. Some of his customers came on their lunch break just to play a couple of games. The pool hall was the entertainment haven for the black men who lived in Chapel Hill. Yea-Yea was a key person in Daddy's pool hall success. When my brothers, sisters, and I were young we called him, "Yeayee," because we could not pronounce his birth name. When Geary attended high school he played football. His friends assumed his family was calling him "Yea-Yea," and that's when he went from "Yeayee" to "Yea-Yea." They thought it went along with his personality as he was always full of excitement, especially on the football field.

Yea-Yea worked with Daddy every day. He learned how to gamble watching Daddy playing nine-ball and poker. Gambling became a habit of my brother as it was for Daddy for many years. The pool hall was usually dimly lit, often hazed over with cigarette smoke. The only lighting was the

Daddy at the pool table

fluorescent light glowing over the green felt covering the pool tables. There was a cold drink and snack machine in the rear of the room. There were very few, if any, females present.

Daddy's customers were usually construction workers on their lunch break, unemployed men who had nothing to do, and others who just had spare time. Daddy and Yea-Yea wore aprons with pockets bulging with quarters to make change for customers who were to the point of "breaking" dollar bills. They walked around from pool table to pool table, racking balls as they grabbed the quarters that were tossed onto them. When the balls were racked the aprons struck the sides of the tables as they hustled from one table to the next to rack balls and make change.

The language was often crass and loud as well, with challenges being yelled from customer to customer, especially if you had a shark (very good player) in the house. One could easily lose fifteen to twenty dollars in a very short time, much of which went into Daddy's apron pocket. Like any other vice, shooting pool can become addictive. You see, Daddy was not only a hustler, but a businessman, and he knew what was one man's loss was another man's gain—HIS!

Every year Daddy drove north of Chapel Hill to the countryside to sell his food at a carnival-type event that was set up by the local black citizens of neighboring Alamance County. Norma, Yea-Yea, and Joe thought Daddy had taken his hustling to the extreme. The tent carnival was down a long narrow dirt road. When Daddy drove through the pothole-filled road his car bounced around splashing muddy water onto the side of the road. Joe was terrified when he went along; however, he had no choice in the matter. Daddy took whoever he wanted to accompany him. None of us liked going to help him with this event, but he was always eager to hustle to make his dollars. He used us as backup when he needed help, handing him canned soft drinks, potato chips, and candy bars as customers ordered them.

Mama and her many jobs made things even better. We moved to a house on the corner of Church and McMaster Streets. Mr. Marvin Norwood, a well-known brick mason in town was the owner of all of the houses on the block. He and his wife lived in a new brick house at the end of the dead-end. We moved into 100 McMaster Street, a much newer house than the one we lived in as small children. This was Mr. and Mrs. Norwood's first home. The house had a cement porch on the front that was the length of the house, with a carport. There was a rock wall across the front yard with bumblebee bushes similar to the ones that I remembered on Merritt Mill Road. Patches of grass were missing from the yard, and I knew there were kids before us who played kick ball—no grass could survive kick ball. Just inside the front door of our house was the living room. A door to the right led to Daddy and Mama's bedroom and in the very back was a tiny room that was used as a bedroom where Norma slept. The only bathroom we had was in the back also. Straight ahead from the living room was the dining room that we used as a family room where we watched TV. The door to the right of the family room led to the bedroom where the other four girls slept, finally with two beds. In the very back of the house toward the back yard was a bedroom for the boys. The kitchen had room enough for Mama to cook her big holiday meals. We were all excited when we finally moved in.

After we settled in the house my sisters and I met Mr. Norwood's grandchildren. Every year they came down from Bronx, New York to spend the summer in a safe environment with their grandparents. "Sugar" was a beautiful girl with long wavy hair down to her shoulders. She was about my age; her brother and sister were a bit younger. When she smiled her dimples stood out and enhanced her perfectly shaped lips. When I first met them they were not happy about coming to a rural environment. When my sisters and I got to know them better, they were excited about coming down to North Carolina every summer to have fun with friends their age.

There were lots of kids in our new neighborhood. Some of them came from down the street and were always standing around looking at us. As a matter of fact, anything we did they were looking. I could not understand why they were staring at us all of the time.

One afternoon Mama decided she was going to cook hamburgers and hot dogs on the grill in our front yard. Growing up, my siblings and I continued to pay attention to Mama when she cooked, and she was our so-called home education teacher. We were accustomed to eating all kinds of delicious foods she prepared. She placed the hamburgers and hot dogs on the grill. The smoke from the charcoal sent an aroma throughout the neighborhood that char-grilled food was being prepared.

By then I noticed faces through the bushes beside our house peeking to see what was going on in our yard. When they saw that we noticed them they jerked back and hid. When they thought we were not looking they peeked again. We began to eat as fast as Mama was taking the food off of the grill. I nudged Mama and whispered, "Look over there." She looked up and smiled. She saw the kids hanging around our yard and finally she said, "Ya'll c'mon, have a hotdog or hamburger." None of them said a word, they were just happy to get some of our food.

Their faces lit up to know that this lady was going to share her food with them. My brothers, sisters, and I became good friends with these kids too. After that, all of the kids in the neighborhood wanted to join in our cookouts. Eventually, they turned into neighborhood cookouts. Every time Mama grilled out she made sure that she cooked enough for all of the children. Some of them had never eaten food that was grilled and served outside while sitting around in the yard having fun. Again, Mama's hosting skills led her family toward continuing our "neighborhood bonding" relationships.

I remembered a few of these kids because they always came to school late. They came to school about two hours late and then their mama came walking up the street to the school with several dogs following her. She always carried a stick with a piece of wire lodged at the end. Soon afterwards the kids and their mama were seen walking back down the street toward home. Their mama had a mental disorder that her children had to endure throughout their childhood until she was put in a facility to get help. She eventually died from her illness. Their father remarried a woman with four children. He had five and together they had two more. There were eleven people living in a three bedroom house. I could relate to this. They learned how to make the best of what they had just as my parents did and their step-mother was a very good cook. She made large pots of homemade vegetable soup that she shared with me. Boy, it was delicious! Not that many folks' cooking could compare with my mama's.

One of our neighbors had a pear tree in her front yard. Her son, "Big Larry," used to climb and shake the limbs and the biggest pears that I had ever seen fell from the tree all over the ground. Anyone who wanted pears joined in and waited for him to shake limb after limb. Sometimes the pears fell down so fast and hard that they hit us on the head. Every time we took pears, his mama would come to the door yelling at him while he was still in the tree, "Laaarrreee, Laaarrreee!" She stood there hanging her head outside the screen door when she realized what was happening, and said "Get out that tree and don't let me catch you back up there again!" That did not keep kids in the neighborhood from taking pears from her tree. If we did not eat them they just fell on the ground and they would rot—we were not about to let that happen. I always got caught along with the other kids in the neighborhood in her pear tree, even after she told us not to.

One day I remember sneaking into her yard to find some pears that were lying on the ground. I noticed that there was white powdered stuff all over the tree. She had sprinkled baking flour on the pear tree so that the kids would think that the pears were no longer edible. I got the pears along with some other kids anyway, took them back home, and washed them off. I knew that she was not going to harm kids, especially her own, over some pears that she didn't even want. After the pears were gone, we had to wait until the next year to try again.

We had other set of neighbors who were fishermen. I remember one of them was raising two of their granddaughters. I was happy to meet them because they were my age. My sisters and I sometimes hung out next door at their house. My family didn't meet many strangers. Mama made every effort to build relationships with the people in our community. One day their grandmother fried "creek fish" that she and her husband caught while fishing early that morning. She fried them in a cast iron frying pan with peanut oil on an old wood burning stove that she had sitting in her back yard. I never saw a person cook on a stove outside. She made a bread-like batter, adding sugar, and called it sweet bread. She baked it in the oven until it was golden brown. When she was finished cooking her meal, she asked me, "Have you ever tried sweet bread?" "No Ma'am!" "Won't cha try some sweet bread?" I said, "Yes, Ma'am." When I took a bite of the sweet bread I thought, "This tastes like my mama had baked it." That's why my siblings and I checked out every family that lived in our neighborhood, and Mama made sure everybody knew us.

Mama's father, Ed Cotton was one of the first deacons at Hamlet Chapel CME Church in Pittsboro, NC where he also ministered for many years. Most of Mama's "kinfolk" are from the Chatham County area. Her home place is at the end of Pleasant Court off of Mann's Chapel Road. My family attended Hamlet after we moved. No matter what it took, Mama was going to make sure that her children could get to Sunday school. The church had an old retired school bus painted white that came to our neighborhood to pick up kids to attend Sunday school. By this time it seemed that Mama was the neighborhood chairperson. She asked most of the parents in the neighborhood to let their children join hers and attend Hamlet Chapel Church for Sunday school.

Mama was so excited about the kids in our neighborhood going to Sunday school that she signed her children up to join the choir. I was mad—I knew that I couldn't even carry a tune. "Why am I doing this?" I thought. "Why can't I draw, make posters, or do something that I am good at?" I hated standing up in front of people. I remembered back to St. Paul's church when I forgot my sentence to recite in Sunday school. Now she wanted me to sing for everyone at church! This was a joke to my brothers, sisters, and me. During church service when it was time to sing I held my head down and hid behind other children so that the congregation could not see my whole face. We had to sing—I could not sing—I hated singing, but Mama didn't care; we had to do it anyway. One day while sitting in the choir stand I looked around at the other children and thought, "All Mama wants to do is to put us on showcase. She knew we couldn't sing, but I guess she was determined to show off her well-dressed children."

Mama also knew we made the choir. If she took us out I believe there would have only been two kids left to sing. I was tall and I had to stand on the top riser and of course "Dip youngins" had to be on the end of each section. I just didn't want to be there, and I thought the choir director was rigid because she pushed us too hard to learn songs. We had to take the bus on Saturdays and ride all the way through the countryside to choir practice. Many days I felt like I was riding on the back of Uncle Jim's truck because the bus was old and raggedy. As soon as we arrived at church the choir leader made us practice for hours at a time. I wanted to be home enjoying time with my friends. She didn't seem to care and all she knew was that she had to prepare a group of kids to sing some songs on Sunday at church.

As soon as church was over on Sunday some of the elderly women asked Mama if I was the one they called "Mary Minor." "Here we go again," I thought. Often I'm asked, "Which one of Dip's youngin's are you?" "I'm not Mary Minor, I'm not Neecy, I'm not a Dip youngin, my name is Annette," I mumbled to myself. I wanted to be called by my name. At the time it was too bad Mama didn't make us name tags to wear when she took us to church and family reunions. There were just too many of us and it seemed like nobody could remember our names.

At homecoming time we were at church all day long. The only thing that made me want to stay was that after church service dinner was served out on the lawn. Mama's food was the most popular on the tables and my brothers, sisters, and I were not about to miss the treat. As a matter of fact, back then it was the only day that I really enjoyed going to church.

Mama stayed up late preparing her meal so that the next morning she would only have to warm it. She cooked fresh white corn with lima beans that were hulled the day before. Roast pork and fried chicken were her main dishes. Mama got up early to fry chicken so that it would be fresh and crispy. She also cooked fresh turnip greens that her cousin Polly let her pick from their garden, potato salad, chittlin's, rolls, sweet potato pie, George Washington fruit cake, and her famous pound cake with lemon frosting drizzling down the sides.

We had to help Mama pack her meal in the trunk of the car. Mama said, "Joe Nathan, get the cooler so we can stop to get some ice and sodas." Off we went down the countryside toward the church with the aroma from the packed food seeping from the trunk through the inside of the car. After we pulled up into the church grounds it was time for the church service to begin. The food was left in the trunk until afterwards. The old wooden tables were lined up from one end of the church yard to the other with plastic white tablecloths. Cars were lined up all over the place, parked on the side of the road and at the back of the church close to the graves.

Homecoming was the biggest day of the year for Hamlet. After the church service was over, everyone bailed out the front door to get to their cars to unpack their boxes and baskets of food. The food was spread out on the tables. My brothers, sisters, and I carried food from the trunk of our car to the table for Mama. Meanwhile, she was busy spreading her lovely flowered tablecloth to cover her section of the table. It was important to Mama that her part of the table was inviting and beautiful. Then Mama arranged her prepared dishes on the table.

Most of the folks who knew Mama walked up to her to let her know that they wanted to sample her food. My brothers, sisters, and I began to worry that we were not going to get any of Mama's food, since she was always generous. People ate some of her food and told her over and over again how wonderful her dishes tasted. Mama said "Thank you" so many times with the biggest smile on her face that I had ever seen. People loved her food and "love" is the main ingredient used when she is cooking.

One time during our teenage years, my sisters and I decided that we wanted our friends to enjoy our food just as others had enjoyed Mama's at our neighborhood cookouts and at church. It was in the summertime when we created the wildest picnics and invited some of the girls in the neighborhood to join us. We were always the ones with the food. It was real cool; we still had our cotton candy machine from when we were little girls that we had gotten for Christmas years ago when we lived on Merritt Mill Road. We did not have any more colored sugar that came with the cotton candy machine. We used regular sugar from Mama's canister and made plain cotton candy. We popped popcorn and poured it in a brown paper sack. We also made Kool-Aid, prepared peanut butter sandwich crackers wrapped in wax paper, and gathered all kinds of junk food that we could find in our kitchen. Everything was put in a cardboard box and off we went walking up McMaster Street to the old Northside school building that the county was using for health clinics.

After we found a place along side of the building that was low enough for us to climb to get on the roof we handed the box of goodies to the first person on top. Then one by one the rest of us climbed up on the roof of the building. We walked and sometimes had to jump from building to building to find the perfect spot for our picnic without the police catching us.

When we heard the rumble of any car someone yelled, "Get down, the cops," but nothing stopped us from enjoying our day even if it took a little longer to get settled. If we were caught I knew what the deal was going to be like with Mama. She was not going to have her children misbehaving. Daddy always yelled at us, but Mama still whupped us. By the time we were settling down for our picnic we'd spread out our blanket and took our goodies out of the box. The cotton candy had melted to almost half its size, the ice had melted in the Kool-Aid, but everything else was okay and our so-called picnic was on. When we were done eating, we packed up our trash and jumped from building to building to find our way back down.

Often a gang of us kids walked through the woods at the back of our neighborhood to find the short cut to the park. We loved to push each other on the swings and sometimes we stood up on our feet and swung. Afterwards we took off our shoes and walked along the shallow edge of the creek in our bare feet. We all moaned as the cold water seeped above our toes covering our ankles. We sometimes brought along empty jars to collect tadpoles, bringing them back home to feed them and, if possible, watch them grow into frogs. Most of the time there were no frogs and the dead tadpoles had to be tossed out into the bushes.

We were always up to something even if it meant walking up the street to the neighborhood house. The house was a recreational center that kids in the community could visit to get help with homework after school. We also participated in recreational activities like dances on the weekends. The neighborhood house provided a place for kids so that they could stay out of trouble and remain safe. Most of the kids in the surrounding area came out and danced the evening away. Mama encouraged her kids to participate because it was a good way to keep us focused. Our neighborhood was the community and our neighbors were a part of our family. The neighborhood house was the thing to do until we found out about the parties on the UNC campus at the dorms.

When students at the university came back to school in the fall, there was always a lot of partying going on through-out the semester, until it was time for the winter break. When we found out about the first party, we had connections to find out about potential parties. Mama let us go out but she gave us a curfew that we sometimes broke. She thought that we were at the neighborhood house, but we would have walked all the way down Franklin Street and across campus by the football stadium, sometimes in the freezing cold, just to party. We thought it was worth every step.

We never got cold, especially on the way back, because we were sweating from the heat that was generated from the packed room of partygoers. Our shirts were soaked with sweat and the heat from our bodies which produced steam as we rushed home to beat our curfew. I remember on one occasion we got home at 1:30 in the morning. Mama was standing right there waiting when we opened the front door. The first thing she told us was that we could not go to bed. "Stay up, seems like ya'll want to stay up all night anyway!" she screamed. Even though we were tired, we had to clean the house for the rest of the morning, and bed was the last thing on our minds. We didn't like it, but it was better than being whupped.

Love what you do, and others will love you for it.

The Foundation of Building the "Dip" Legacy

At this time Mama's full-time job was at the UNC Hospital in the Central Supply Department. Her job was to sterilize instruments, tools, and equipment used in procedures. Most days Mama took a cab to work unless Daddy had time to drop her off. Taking the car was out of the question because parking was limited at the hospital. Sometimes in the evening I rode with Daddy to pick Mama up from work, especially on her payday. When Daddy approached the area where Mama worked she was sitting along the brick wall waiting for him to come. When she saw our red station wagon approaching she walked toward us and got in the front seat of the car.

Every two weeks on Friday, Daddy took Mama to the bank so that she could take care of her financial business, while we sat in the car and waited. I was always excited about Mama coming back to the car since payday was my chance to ask her for some money. When she got back in the car I was hanging over the front seat. When Daddy drove off, I asked Mama, "Would you give me a dollar?" She answered, "I don't have a dollar." I could not believe what I had just heard. I slid back into my seat and I thought to myself, "How could she not have any money? She just got paid today." Mama always put her paycheck in the bank so she could help Daddy pay bills. When she needed cash she always asked Daddy. He was the cash man, always walking around with a big wad of money in his pocket.

As far back as I can remember Daddy carried a pistol in his pocket, even though he never had to use it. He was always prepared to protect his family just as any father would. My family's safety was his job. Sometimes at home he laid his pistol on the table in the living room. He didn't lay his pistol around on purpose. Many nights after leaving the pool hall late he was merely exhausted. However, I was terrified of his pistol and I wanted to make sure that it was not about to discharge. I didn't think that it would but I was being safe. I made sure that I was not in the way of a bullet. I ran past it to get to the other side of the room. Daddy was not about to let anybody rob him of his hard-earned dollars.

While my grandparents were operating Bills BBQ, Daddy created a rolling restaurant, driving his station wagon around to construction sites and repair shops selling food. When there wasn't enough room in the station wagon he began borrowing one of Grandpa's vans as his route had increased. Daddy taught a neighbor how to prepare the food. For breakfast he sold country ham, sausage, bacon, and egg biscuits. The sandwiches were wrapped with thick plastic wrap and then rubbed across a heated pan to seal. Grits were sold in small Styrofoam cups with butter already melted on them, and piping hot fresh coffee was sold by the cup.

There was also junk food like potato chips, Snickers, Almond Joy, Baby Ruth, chewing gum, and miscellaneous items like tobacco and cigarettes. Sometimes my sisters and I had to keep the potato chip rack, candy, and gum shelf filled. We also had to separate the salt and pepper packets that sometimes got tossed around in the box when Daddy turned curves. Pint cartons of milk and canned drinks were packed in a cooler filled with ice.

In our kitchen Daddy, Norma, and Mrs. Charlie Mae prepared the breakfast food every morning. While Daddy was out on the breakfast run, they prepared BBQ sandwiches, hotdogs, and cheeseburgers. Chicken parts were fried in a huge cast iron frying pan and sold as white meat and dark meat sandwiches. Some chicken dinners were also prepared with mashed potatoes and gravy, green beans, and rolls. When Daddy returned from his breakfast run the lunch items were ready to go. Sometimes if he got back early enough he'd help prepare lunch.

Later on he became so popular with his rolling restaurant that our family's name spread around town. Most of the construction companies looked forward to him serving meals to their workers. Daddy's restaurant on wheels was growing and that's when he purchased a step van. He also purchased an aluminum oven that he had welded inside so that it would be stationary. The oven had five drawers and each was heated with sterno. Daddy finally had a place to keep food hot, so he began to make different kinds of complete dinners for lunch from the recipes that Mama used to cook at home—meat loaf, fresh fish, BBQ chicken, and stewed beef.

All dinners were piping hot and stacked on our kitchen table so that when Daddy returned from breakfast everything was set to go. He seldom returned with leftovers. Daddy was very pleased with how the business was moving forward.

Bill Council

Daddy was a very good cook. Sometimes when he had time he would cook us breakfast for dinner—country ham grilled in a cast iron fry pan, with gravy from its natural juices, fresh apples baked with butter, brown sugar and cinnamon, grits and biscuits. Whenever Daddy decided to cook for his family it was a special treat.

By this time Bill had graduated from high school and he followed Daddy's footsteps to serve in the military. He joined the Army and was stationed in the Panama Canal. Bill was the only family member who didn't experience the startup of building Daddy and Mama's legacy at Bill's BBQ. He was always the intelligent eager sibling. He loved learning and has always had a balanced life. He was dubbed "funny world" in high school. He was humorous and the center of attention of every conversation he had. His friends always wanted to be in his presence. He is a well liked gentleman with hundreds of friends. He is fun to be around and everyone in the world would love him if they met him.

The following year Bon and Lane finished high school and they took turns driving the standard gear step van; both of them could drive it as if it were a small car. When Lane drove she'd whip the van around the curve. You could barely see her head if you looked through the back window. Her legs stretched to their limit as she sat close to the edge of the driver's seat to touch the gas and brake pedals. They rode with the side doors open as they drove around town and sometimes toward Durham.

On their first stop at the Chevrolet dealership they pulled the van around the back of the building. Lane jumped out of the van to prop the back doors open. Bon taped the handwritten menu to the backside of the van where Daddy had built a counter at the back of the van to set orders on for the customers. A large cooler was used to keep drinks cold with lots of ice piled on top.

Sometimes during the summer when I went with them my hands froze from digging down inside the cooler to find a drink that we were almost sold out of. This was the time that I learned to count change without an adding machine or cash register. I started out a little slow but I caught on quickly. I continued to use the same process as I did when I was learning my multiplication tables. If I was going to help work the truck I needed to have a calculator in my head. Daddy was used to counting money in his head and he could do it really fast. My brothers and sisters and I also had to learn to count money fast. Customers were served and then we were off to the next stop. There was no time wasted because each stop had a scheduled time.

When the van pulled up to construction sites, men came from all over the place, from inside and outside and from around the back of incomplete framed constructions. The workers formed a line that had at least thirty hungry men waiting for Daddy's food. Most of the workers came without shirts and their backs were tanned dark brown from the heat of summer. They loved our menu items and every week day some workers even waited outside before our van pulled up. Daddy was not going to let them down, because we were always there. He taught all his children how to manage the van so that it could go out every day.

This is the time when Mama quit her job at the hospital and my parents were operating Bill's BBQ. They were eager to continue my grandparents' legacy when they retired. Grandpa had run out of energy and had heart trouble, and Grandma was just plan tired of the restaurant business. Both of my grandparents thought that they were at an age where they were old enough to retire. My parents were qualified to take over the business due to the many years of experience working at Bill's BBQ and the building of their own food delivery business.

This was a good time for both of my grandparents to let go and let my parents run the business. Daddy and Mama began planning their restaurant; making decisions on how they were going to run it. This was Mama's chance to do her thing with the help of Daddy. Customers finally were going to have a chance to buy food that Mama had created with her recipes for many years. Mama knew she had to make the best of this moment. Everyone around town knew that she was an excellent self-taught "dump" cook. She cooked almost anything that was edible and called it traditional country cooking. Mama used the same weekly menu that she made up for our family at home to create daily specials at the restaurant.

One day her special was country style steak. She made brown gravy with the remaining oil and the crumbs from the meat, stirring in flour and adding water. She smothered the gravy over the steak and mashed potatoes. Cabbage seasoned with pork was included. Fresh fish was always served on Fridays with buttered potatoes simmered with chopped onions, fresh turnip greens, and hushpuppies.

Mama learned how to create her own BBQ sauce recipe. Daddy added more drivers to the delivery end of the business and delivered boxed meals around town, mostly on campus where the students lived. Most of the delivered meals on campus were fried chicken boxed meals with French fries and slaw. The university was big business for Bill's BBQ.

Daddy and Mama worked along with their children for many years and were successful making a good living. Mama hired her sister, my aunt Bernice, because she was a good cook, too. Both of them had worked at the Hollywood Grill that my uncle Jim once owned. Most of the other help that worked for Grandpa were kept on Daddy and Mama's payroll. They had been employed for many years and were dedicated hard workers. Everybody in our family pitched in to help continue the restaurant's legacy that my grandparents started.

The restaurant had a juke box, a toilet in the ladies' and men's restrooms and an old hand sink in the hallway with a

Family members in grandparents' backyard and Bill's BBQ.

Dip at Bill's BBQ—hot dogs: 45¢

pull down cloth towel to dry your hands. My parents did a little redecorating. The bathrooms were repainted and the hand sink was replaced. The jukebox was replaced with an up-to-date one that took a quarter and played two songs.

There was a counter with five seats where customers could sit down and eat or order takeout. The menu was similar to my grandparents' with more items. It consisted of fried chicken sandwiches, BBQ sandwiches, hushpuppies with chopped onions sticking out of the crust, pinto beans in a carton with a scoop of chili and raw chopped onions on top, chicken giblets with necks and noodles, hot dogs with real homemade chili, numerous dinner meals, and our famous Big Bill's Burger. Most blue collar workers ordered takeout during lunchtime and sat in their town trucks or company trucks with the doors open under a shade tree on the side of the restaurant.

The back of the restaurant had a small BBQ pit house and in the very back was a storage room with mostly boxes. My sisters and I continued to fold "chicken boxes." We were no longer paid a penny for each one—we were paid a daily rate for working. All employees helped load up the van for Daddy to go to UNC football games just as Grandpa had. This is when I got my chance to work for dollars. I didn't realize that working for dollars was going to require so much of my time. As a result I became tired and sometimes I just wanted to stay at home.

One day a couple of guys came in the restaurant and both of them ordered Big Bill's Burgers. The burgers were prepared with two hamburger patties with seasoned salt sprinkled on them while they were cooking, two slices of cheese, and when the burgers were done we added Mama's special sauce, lettuce and tomato, sliced grilled onions, pickle slices, and hot peppers. The sandwiches were given to the guys without the meat by mistake. I didn't even notice it until they were down the street and out of sight. I ran out the door to see if I could catch the guys, but it was too late.

"They are gone!" I panicked saying to Norma who was working with me on this particular day. She said, "Oh my God! They are going to be so mad with us!" A few days later one of them came back in the restaurant to buy hot dogs and we told him that we forgot to put the burgers on their sandwiches. He said, "We didn't even miss them and they were the best sandwiches we'd ever had." Norma and I laughed because we knew the real reason why they didn't miss the burgers. The flavor of Mama's recipe and the hot peppers consumed them as they ate the sandwiches. Whose burgers could be delicious without the meat? My mama's.

I remember at the end of each business day when the cash was counted, the sales tax amount was removed and set aside. At the end of the night when I was helping Daddy and Mama clean up the restaurant, they said to me that this money is not ours. They didn't include the sales tax in their operating bank account; it was deposited into a separate account. They paid the North Carolina Department of Revenue monthly sales tax that was collected. Just watching my parents handle the monetary end of their business ignited my interest in accounting.

A few years went by and business was booming. Daddy and Mama's relationship began to go down hill. This was not the first time Daddy had stayed out all night and not come home. Mama felt like she was doing most of the hard work while Daddy was somewhere gambling. He worked very hard at Bill's BBQ during the day so that he could take care of his family, but his love for gambling and playing poker got in the way of family. My daddy was a pool shark and a lot of the men constantly challenged him many days to play nine-ball. Therefore, he didn't resist the temptation.

Daddy's friend knew how good he was at playing pool. The gambling turned into an overnight game on many occasions and sometimes my daddy would be gone for a couple of days. Every day was not a winning day and losing money was not what my family needed.

Year after year, when he finally came home he was exhausted to the extent that all he could do was sleep. If Mama needed to ask him to do anything he verbally went off and they would get into a fight. Both of my parents were tired when they got off work, sometimes making situations that weren't that bad turn into an argument. Daddy didn't want Mama telling him how to make money when he knew he was doing it for his family. Mama wanted Daddy to make money, but she also wanted him home at night. It amazes me now when I reflect back; most of the time I never missed Daddy when he was not at home.

There were days that my brothers, sisters, and I had to listen to my Daddy and Mama fuss and fight until one day she went over to Aunt Bernice's house for a few days. My aunt was there for Mama when she needed comfort and a place to go for relief from Daddy. However, I could not believe Mama had left us kids at home by ourselves. Norma again had to step up and play Mama's role. Mama needed time to get herself together concerning how she was going to handle Daddy's attitude about only coming home occasionally. We spent all day on Saturday and Sunday at Aunt Bernice's house with Mama so that she would have some time with us. We knew that she was going to face Daddy eventually. I said to Mama, "When are you coming home?" She said, "I don't know right now."

*Family birthday parties
with the grandkids.*

Things were different around the house without Mama. I didn't have to eat any green vegetables, because most of the food that Norma made for us everybody liked. When Mama came back home after a few days things got back to normal for our family. Business went on as usual despite the temporary separation; Mama was not going to let anything get in the way of her dream.

During the years that we lived on McMaster Street, seven of my nieces and nephews were born. No matter what, my family had each other, and to me we resembled a basketball team. Daddy and Mama were our coaches, my brothers, sisters, and I were the team players, and the grandkids were the screaming cheerleaders. With all of us, when there was a birthday to celebrate we didn't invite other people since there were plenty of us to have fun and enjoy each other's company. However, Mama's house was a community all by itself as it continued to grow day by day, and our house was also the neighborhood hangout.

It's okay to let them see you sweat. Success is tough.

My College Debut

I was in my final year of high school and Joe was still living in Louisville. I was excited about moving forward and making my college debut. I took a bookkeeping class to fulfill my elective requirement for my senior year at Chapel Hill High School. This gave me a chance to use what I had learned from watching Daddy and Mama managing money in their business. I did not think much about the class when I signed up—all I knew was that I needed additional credits to graduate from high school—June, 1974.

The day after the first bookkeeping test I noticed the teacher was standing outside the door greeting the students while they were entering the classroom. When I approached the classroom door, Mrs. Young informed me that I had scored the highest grade on the test, and she just wanted to congratulate me before the class began. I knew that I had passed the test, but I did not think I had "aced" it.

While I was taking the test I applied the "Daddy and Mama" business principles that I observed on a daily basis working at Bill's BBQ. I knew what debits and credits were— I also knew what it meant to balance a cash register and a bank statement. I went inside the class and took my seat. When Mrs. Young handed me my test paper I realized that I had made a 103—A+. My eyes lit up as my eyebrows rose. I was surprised that I had gotten everything right, even the bonus problem for extra credit. I was ecstatic with my grade. After class Mrs. Young told me that she thought that I should consider becoming an accountant. Throughout high school I had always thought about being a social worker. While I was walking down the hallway to my next class I took into consideration what she had said to me. For several days I continued to think about accounting as my profession. The thought just wouldn't go away—I wasn't sure. "What should I do?—What I love or what I am good at?" Mama always talked about family, community, and how important it is to help others. I felt that social work was my purpose in life working with people in communities and making the town where I grew up better. I had already experienced building relationships in my neighborhood and church—as far as I was concerned I was ready to be a social worker.

I remembered how Mama made people feel like family. She helped people in any way that she could and every day that she could. Even though I was pretty good at bookkeeping and I loved numbers, I thought, "What should I do with myself?" After graduation and during the summer before I was college bound, I decided to major in accounting.

I continued to work at Bill's BBQ so I could save money to for college. I went to Belk's in Chapel Hill almost every day looking for clothes and shoes on sale. I bought most of my clothes on "Hot Diggity Day." This was a day in Chapel Hill when most of the stores and shops downtown had huge sales, which were advertised in the newspapers and on the radio. Everybody in town would be waiting for "Hot Diggity Day."

The crowd, along with my sisters and I, stood outside the stores on a Saturday morning anxiously waiting to get inside. We stood at the upstairs back door of the Belk's building since we wanted to get to the section with the clothes first and then we wanted to find the TV that was on sale for one dollar—everybody else did too. A lot of items were on sale for less than five dollars. There were free donuts and fountain Coca-Cola. The fresh aroma of popcorn for the customers filled the air outside of the main entrance. When the doors were unlocked, everyone started pushing to get inside. Actually, the momentum of the crowd moved us inside of the store without much effort on our part. We all were like scavengers, searching to find as many items of clothing and shoes as possible—on sale. Afterwards, I couldn't wait to get home to spread my bargains on my bed and count my pieces. Weeks before the sale I already had a box of clothes, shoes, and toiletries that I had begun collecting for college. Soon after I got home and admired my bargains, I grabbed an armful and dumped them into my box. I was definitely ready for college and singing around the house "Elizabeth City State, I'm comin' to do my thang!" By this time I knew that I was going to study to become an accountant.

It was an early Sunday morning when Daddy, Mama, Spring, and I packed the car with all of my belongings. Daddy drove us down NC 58 East toward Elizabeth City where I would be attending college. Roy had previously graduated from Elizabeth City back in the sixties when it was only a teacher's college. I sat in the back seat of the car holding onto the door handle as my hand created sweat from my tight grip. I observed the signs posted along the roadway as Daddy drove through one small town after another. I was happy about going to college—I also thought about how I was leaving home for the first time without a family member.

My family was our own little neighborhood and most of the time we were together. The closer we got to Elizabeth City the more I felt my family bond coming to an end. This was a scary feeling for me as I had to adjust to independence—I felt somewhat uneasy about being able to make my own decisions now. Mama was the decision maker and that was what I was accustomed to.

I began to feel like I was going to miss my family too much, in spite of the sound of Mama screaming out her children's names—especially mine, "Neeeeeeeeeeeeecy." I couldn't believe that I was going to miss my mama's screaming voice. I was used to it but it was okay now as it was about to end. I thought a lot about what my upcoming college experience was going to be like along the way. Before I knew it, Daddy was passing the sign, "Welcome to Elizabeth City." Finally the time was about to come as we approached the university.

After about a four hour trip we arrived at Bias Hall dormitory for girls where I would be living for the next nine months. When I got out of the car—I smelled this awful odor that filled the air. "Oh my God! What's that smell?" I said while Daddy laughed at me and explained that the smell was from the pulp mills. I thought to myself, "Okay, it will go away soon and I will be alright."

Daddy and Spring helped me take my things to the second floor to find my room while Mama came along behind us. When I arrived at my room, my roommate was already there, and I introduced myself to her. She was from Goldsboro, North Carolina. She was a very friendly young lady and she told me where I needed to go to get the things that she already had taken care of which included our orientation schedule for the week.

After we lugged everything up to my room, Spring and I went to pick up linens for my bed from the laundry house across the street from my dorm. We walked across the lawn and some guys were trying to make conversation with us. A basketball player approached us and introduced himself to Spring, then went back to sit under the tree with the rest of his buddies. At this time my sister was still in high school and would be returning home. I thought, "If he thinks that he's gonna get a date, he's in for a shock." Afterwards, we met Daddy and Mama back at my room. Daddy then drove us to the finance office to pay the bill for my tuition. Daddy was the "cash money man" with his big wad of hundreds as he counted them out on the counter, one by one as the cashier watched him. After he received his receipt Daddy, Mama, and Spring said their goodbyes. I stood watching as they drove away until I could no longer see the car. When I returned to my dorm, all I could think about was, "They left me in a college town with a stinkin' smell."

The next morning I had breakfast with my roommate at 7:30 am prior to classes starting at 8:00 am. While we walked in the cafeteria my nose wrinkled due to that stinkin' smell in the air. I sure did not need to smell this first thing in the morning, especially before I had a chance to eat breakfast. I took tiny steps along the buffet line looking through the steamed glass at the sausage and hash browns; thinking to myself, "This is not what Mama's cooking looks like." I thought maybe I'll try them.

I asked the server for the sausage and hash browns—I knew for sure that I didn't want any of those darn eggs—I didn't even want Mama's. I thought to myself with a puzzled look on my face, "Oh my God! Where is Mama?" I went over to the cold bar to grab a box of Frosted Flakes and a cup for milk. I had to get milk from a dispenser and the first thing I thought, "If this is not real milk, then how in the world am I going to eat my cereal?" Mama was such a good cook and I was spoiled. I realized that her cooking actually made it harder for me to be able to eat somebody else's cooking. I thought, "I'm gonna starve."

I took a container of orange juice and walked out into the dining area. I looked around for a place to sit. I found my roommate in the crowd and I sat down across the table from her. I just sat and stared at the sausage and hash browns thinking, "There is no way in the world I can even think about eating this stuff." Some of the upper-class students from the table across from me noticed that I was not happy with my breakfast. They assured me that I would get used to the food since this is what it was going to be like for four years. Immediately I ignored them, began pouring milk on my cereal and adding a couple spoonfuls of sugar. I loved really sweet cereal since I was a young girl. I ate my cereal leaving the sausage and hash browns—this wouldn't have happened at Mama's table.

I rushed since I had to sign up for my major classes. I had changed my mind again. By this time I decided to major in sociology, because of what Mama had instilled in her children about the importance of family and community. After settling in and getting used to the college routine, things were going along fine. I finally adjusted to the food a little more than I had thought I would. The upper-classmen were right; I was gonna eat the food or I was gonna starve.

Game day was approaching for Elizabeth City's first football game. I was excited about doing something different on the weekend besides hanging around the dorm all day long. On this Saturday morning, I walked out the front door of my dorm with my roommate anticipating catching a ride to the football game.

When I took the last step down to the ground I noticed a lady who stood out in the crowd. She was sitting on the grass with a couple of other people. When I got a little closer I thought to myself, "That's my mama!" I was surprised that Mama came to visit me. She had come for the football game with the parents of one of the players, Michael. His parents grew up in Chatham County where Mama was raised as a young girl. They were at most of his games. Mama thought that she would take a break and come along to surprise me—Mama didn't take breaks. We all went to the game and it was so much fun. I felt brand new because Mama was with me. I wasn't homesick anymore even though I didn't have any of Mama's food.

The first semester was about to come to an end and I was taking my final exams. The time had come for Thanksgiving break. Daddy and Mama sent Bon and Lane to pick me up from school. They brought Bon's daughter, Panda, who was almost two years old. She was born with a rare genetic heart disease; she was frail and hadn't learned to walk. When my sisters arrived I didn't realize that they had been looking for me all over campus.

They wanted to hurry to get back to Chapel Hill. When I finished my last exam and was leaving class, I walked out of the building and "Bam!" there they were. Bon was always in a hurry. She rushed me to get my things so that we could get on the road. Bon said, "C'mon let's go now!" She was almost running—I had to keep up with her and take them to my dorm. She questioned me, "Where have you been?" "I was in class finishing my last exam." I replied.

Then I grabbed my suitcase and put it in the trunk of the car and we were on the road. I sat in the back seat with Panda while Bon drove us back to Chapel Hill. While we were riding, I thought, "Why in the world did Daddy and Mama send Bon to get me?" She didn't have any patience at all!

After a few hours the ride became irritable for little Panda and she began to cry. I tried to soothe and settle her down. That wasn't enough because Panda was getting more irritated—Bon was trying her best to hurry and get us home so that Panda would be more comfortable. We were almost back in Chapel Hill when Panda started to pass out. She had passed out many times before due to her illness. I was scared to death and I thought that I was going to go out of my mind!

Panda was in fact having a seizure. She had had seizures before but this time we were in the middle of rush hour traffic. Bon was trying to get through the traffic to get Panda to the hospital emergency room at UNC in Chapel Hill. When we arrived the doctors and nurses rushed to grab Panda from Bon's arms. Lane and I jumped back in the car, drove to the restaurant to get Mama and tell her what happened. When we arrived at Bill's BBQ all we could say was "Mama come, Panda is at the emergency room." Mama hurried to the car and Lane drove us back to the hospital. When we arrived at the hospital the news that we were about to hear was devastating. Panda had passed away because her heart, lungs, and liver had enlarged due to her condition. This moment was extremely sad. "How could something like this happen so quickly?—Especially in the car when I was coming home from school?" We were terribly saddened by Panda's death and I was glad that Bon had family by her side during this time.

Panda's death was a shock to my family. The doctors never informed my sister that Panda's condition was life

Panda's first birthday party

threatening. I thought that Panda would cope and live with her illness as many other children did. Planning her funeral was the next stage of this unexpected death. The same funeral home that my family once lived near and grew up around was called to take her precious tiny body away from the morgue. When it was time for us to view her body I slowly took steps going up to the door of Bynum Weaver's funeral home. Ironically, I was having flashbacks of when I was a young girl when my brothers, sisters, and I made sure we viewed every dead person at the funeral home. This time it was no joke. Our names were signed because we were family; it was for real this time. Death had hit home—this time it was Daddy and Mama's granddaughter—my sister's daughter and my niece.

Panda's body lay as if she was sleeping in a small white casket. She wore a beautiful flowered pink and purple dress, her tiny earrings, and her sterling silver African bangles on her wrist. While I was standing next to Bon she decided to rearrange the bangles on Panda's wrist. When she did, the bangles left an indentation in her skin. Bon immediately placed the bangles back. Panda was laid to rest a couple days later.

After the funeral it was time for me to go back to college. Mama called Michael's parents and asked them if I could ride back to school with him. Of course, they said yes, and Michael became my ride back and forth for the rest of the school year so that my family wouldn't have to drive so far.

Returning to school was not the same any more. I felt that my classes were extremely easy, and it was not challenging enough. The atmosphere with the students was disappointing. I found out as time went by that a certain few of them elected to cheat, and this was not my style. I worked my "butt" off for my grades and didn't understand why someone would take advantage of their educational opportunity.

The environment of the university was quite different from what I was used to. The university was located in an area that didn't offer the things that I was accustomed to in Chapel Hill. I loved to shop and there weren't any specialty stores or boutiques in the area. I also didn't particularly like the dormitory atmosphere. I couldn't believe that there were girls that actually asked me if they could wear my clothes. And I thought, "What the hell? I spent a lot of money for my clothes—get your ass on!" From the time my siblings and I started earning money from working at the restaurant we were solely responsible for buying our own clothes. There was no way that I was going to lend any of my things to anyone. These weren't Mama's clothes—they were mine!

I was not at college for any other reason than to obtain an education. I truly was not interested in the party scene, dating, or really anything else for that matter. I was simply bored with the college life. I was sick and tired of that stinking foul smell that never went away from the pulp. I needed to be where I could enjoy Mama's food any time I wanted, and I missed my family. I decided that I no longer wanted to attend college at Elizabeth City State.

About eleven o'clock one night, I called home and asked to speak to Mama. As soon as she got on the phone I begged, "Hey Mama, plllllleeeeeeeeasssse come and get me now!" Mama said, "What in the world is wrong?" I replied, "I am ready to leave this place and by the time you get here I will have all of my things packed and ready to go." I didn't even give it a second thought that by the time Mama drove four hours to pick me up it would be almost five o'clock in the morning. Mama said, "Calm down, what in the world could be so bad that you have to leave right now?" I pleaded, "Pllllllllleeeeeeeeeeasssssse come and get me?" Mama said, "Complete your freshman year and start looking for another college." *Click.* That was the end of our conversation.

The very next day I wrote a letter to North Carolina Central University requesting an application for enrollment. I received my application the next week and I immediately filled it out and mailed it back the same day. About six weeks later, I received a letter stating that I was accepted for enrollment for the next school year. I hung in there the next few months at Elizabeth City State until finally the day came that

I was going back home for the summer. I returned to Chapel Hill in the same big car that brought me to Elizabeth City and I was never going to go hungry again, nor would I be without Mama's food again!

Believe in your dream. It will come true.

There's No Place Like Home

L eaving school and returning back home was going to be a little different. Daddy and Mama had completed building our new home on Piney Mountain Road. Finally, I was going to have a bedroom and possibly a bathroom all to myself. My family was used to living in a three bedroom house with one bathroom. My brothers, sisters, and I had shared bedrooms and a bed for such a long time. Now we had five bedrooms and three bathrooms.

I remembered before going off to college that all of the preparation and getting plans drawn was very exciting for my family. When I got back home Spring was the only child living in our new home. "Where did everybody go?" I thought. It seemed that now that my family had enough room for everybody, they had all moved out of the house before Daddy, Mama, and Spring moved into the new house. It was definitely okay with me. Now I knew that I would have a bathroom to myself. I settled in at home and began to work for my parents at Bill's BBQ. At this time business was still good.

I worked the entire summer. During that time I had to learn how to drive before the school year began so that I could drive to Durham for college. Mama took me to the driver examiner's office so that I could take the test to get my learner's permit and to start practicing how to drive. I was happy about learning how to drive, and I felt the same way I did when I finally learned how to ride a bike "back in the day." Mama agreed to let me drive her everywhere she needed to go.

One day, she said, "Neecy, let's go over to PD's" (her sister Marie's nickname). I drove down Rosemary Street, then onto Starlight Drive, and around the corner to Broad Street to Aunt PD's house. Her house sat beside a little old wooden house with a fence around it and a yard full of children's toys. Aunt PD always came to our house around the holidays to entertain Mama after having a few drinks. She would hug Mama and say, "I love ya Dip," while Mama sat around and laughed at her. My aunt PD was especially funny when she teased Mama, "I'll whip ya' ass Dip!" Uncle Jim came to our house to scare us as children and Aunt PD came to "act out" with Mama.

I often drove Mama over to her house because Mama had a taste for what I thought was unusual cooking—crappy, rabbit, squirrel and "coon!" There were numerous pots on my aunts stove cooking pigs' ears, pigs' feet, and even pigs' tails, known as soul food. Aunt PD cooked a bit different from what I was accustomed to eating. Mama rarely cooked any of these types of critters. I would eat my greens every day for the rest of my life before I could or would eat that stuff.

Mama and her sister loved "soul food," as mentioned above, even though Mama was a traditional country cook. My aunt's house reeked of the stale smell of the cigar smoke that my uncle was puffing or of the ashes lying in the ash tray. The cooking of the different types of game food created a repulsive scent that forced me go outside and sit on the porch with my cousin Peggy for fresh air.

Peggy was born with a learning disability, but was able to work most of her life in a special program. She was the daughter of Mama's sister, Cora, who had passed away when Peggy was a teenager. Aunt PD raised her just as Mama had raised Roy. Without a doubt and without a thought this was true family bonding and that's where community begins.

Mama always took a seat at the kitchen table so that she could get on with Aunt PD's feast. After a while I got the nerve to venture into the kitchen to peek into a couple of pots. When I lifted the lid on a pot my facial expression said it all, as I thought to myself, "Oh my God, who in the world would eat this?" I hurried right back outside holding my breath and took a seat on the porch. Later on I decided to go inside and watch TV while Mama finished eating. Mama was taking too long and I wanted her to hurry up so I could practice driving more.

I drove for about three weeks with Mama on the passenger side. She took me back to the driver examiner's office to take the road test. I was nervous, but desperately wanted to pass, and I did. I was happy about being able to drive by myself. Sometimes Daddy would let me drive the station wagon. Before college was to begin I had to learn how to drive Lane's car that was a four-speed. Lane saved her money and she was the first person in my family to purchase a new car— even before Daddy and Mama. I was shocked that she would let me drive her car, but it was the only transportation available for me to drive at the time.

Even though my siblings and I fussed and fought, my parents thought that we should help each other. Lane showed me what I did not know about driving a standard gear shift car. She hung in there with me every step of the way. She took me driving and let me watch her change the gears, releasing the clutch, and accelerating the gas pedal at the same time without the engine stalling. I drove around the parking lot of the old Northside school so that I could get a feel of what the clutch would feel like to my left foot. I had to get used to using both of my feet to get the car going. When I felt comfortable with the "feet moving thang," I told Lane that I was ready to go out on the road. I sat in the driver's seat and followed her instructions. Lane showed so much patience. Her guidance assisted me as the car jerked and stalled a couple of times. I did pretty well in the beginning keeping my feet in the right place at the right time. After about the tenth time, I had learned enough to drive by myself, but I still had to master hills.

It was almost August and time for college to start and I had learned how to drive a stick shift car. Going up hills was still my biggest challenge. Stopping and taking off on a hill made me very nervous. I had to do this; I had no other way to school. I mapped out my path and thought about all the ways I could go and not have to encounter a hill. I prayed the entire trip to campus—I knew that I was not going to master any hills until I confronted them.

No matter how much I tried to eliminate hills I was going to have to deal with them in order to drive my sister's car. The first day I drove to school for class, things went well. Every hill that I came to I pulled off okay. After that, I no longer felt a need to panic. At the end of my day I drove all the way back home without any problems. I was excited and could not wait to get back and tell Lane how well it went. I let her know how I confronted those hills and mastered them all. She said, "I told you what to do, and you did it—it's easy!" The next day was even better.

The first thing that I did at school was change my major from sociology to accounting. I was now excited to study business. Deciding to go to college close to home was a good thing. I felt that being back around my family's business was in my best interest. I was so excited about my new major I decided to take classes in the summer to get ahead. I got up early every morning and I always was concerned about what I was going to wear. I always loved to dress up since "back in the day" attending Sunday school. I was a neat gal with my pressed clothes, curled hairdo, and particularly my mani-cured nails holding onto my *Glamour* magazine with one arm and my book bag across my shoulder.

Most days during my break between classes I'd go down-stairs in the Commerce Building where there was a snack bar that was operated by a blind couple. I was amazed the first time I went there. There was always a line all the way out the door. The small store reminded me of Mr. Weaver's store when I was in Junior High School. Even though the stacks of items were inside the glass case, they managed to retrieve them—whatever a customer ordered they knew exactly where it was located.

They took ones, fives, and tens. All customers had to do was to tell them what bill they were giving them while the rest of the eager students waiting in line watched in amaze-ment while they checked each and every customer out. They were not worried about people cheating them because the "honor system" meant something back then.

At school this was the place I spent most of my money if I wanted snack items, because anyone who could do what this couple was doing was more than a conqueror to me. Without a doubt they had confidence in who they were and what they were doing.

I have learned a lot in my life from watching others. Mostly, I have learned that the hills that we do not try to climb are the only ones we will always look up at. It's okay to look down, too. It's just a reminder to all of us to realize how steep a climb can be.

Expect the unexpected. It's part of the race.

Mama's Business
Venture

Mama decided that she no longer wanted to be a part of operating Bill's BBQ, my grandparents' legacy. She had always talked about owning her own restaurant, and that day finally came when she began looking around town for a place to build her dream. Mama knew the majority of realtors and construction companies around Chapel Hill. One day, she was approached by Mr. George Tate, a realtor who lived in our neighborhood. He knew the business potential of what Mama could create. He managed several buildings in town, and one of them had previously housed a failed restaurant operated by Mr. Percy Tuck, another well-known business-man. Mr. Tate thought that the Rosemary Street location was a good place for Mama to establish a restaurant.

Mama set a time to meet with Mr. Tate to discuss the pos-sibilities for her business venture. I remember the day when a few family members went with Mama to take a look around to see if the building was suitable for the type of restaurant she was interested in establishing.

Mama was excited about the possibility of renting the building. "Don't worry about the rent." Mr. Tate told her.

"Pay me when business picks up." The building was already furnished with old dirty equipment that was left from the prior tenant, but Mama could visualize the outcome of each piece after it was scrubbed clean.

Everybody followed behind Mr. Tate through the front door and back to the kitchen. The exhaust fan had been shut off for a while, leaving a strong foul odor that was left from spoiled food and grease that had been sitting in the deep fryers for quite some time. Mama said, "Hurry, open the back door!" The building was a very small place, but it was just enough for Mama to get her restaurant started. In fact, the only thing that was needed was a good cleaning before any food could be purchased and stored.

This was definitely a great opportunity for Mama and the thought had lingered in her mind for many years. Mama was aware that sole business ownership meant hard work and that's something she was no stranger to. The thought of actually owning a restaurant meant independence for her, and she knew that it would allow her to use her unique gift—creating recipes.

Food and supplies were the major items needed for startup. Mama signed the lease and then she informed the rest of the family. The day that Mama picked up the key to the restaurant her children flocked behind her back down Rosemary Street to take a closer look around inside the building. We all watched as Mama assessed what her needs were going to be to open the restaurant. We cleaned for weeks. We never thought that a kitchen could be so filthy. Some of us wiped shelves, washed dishes, cleaned ovens and deep fat fryers, while Mama sat in a chair pulled up close to the refrigerator with a bucket of sanitized hot water and a rag to clean it. The bathrooms were sanitized also. The walls in the kitchen were painted white which made the area look much bigger, with a fresh new look. Mama had a set of track lights installed above the work tables to make the kitchen even brighter. It was exciting for my brothers, sisters, and me to be helping Mama set up her restaurant. Four green booths with wood tables and three wood tables with chairs made up the twenty-two seat dining area. All of the tables were draped with plastic brown checkered tablecloths, and we wiped them all clean. After all the wiping and scrubbing came the floors which were mopped and waxed. Although everything still looked worn, the restaurant was spotless.

The restaurant was to be called "Dip's," which is Mama's nickname with "Country Kitchen" on the end to reflect her style of cooking the traditional southern way. People sometimes associate country cooking with "soul food," but Mama was not about to let anyone call her food anything unless it was country cooking. She was always inspired with the traditions of family gathering for daily meals while I was growing up. Mama was not a chef, nor did she want to be known as one. "I am a cook, and there's nothing fancy about my food. It's just good food," she says.

The one thing that Mama was sure of was that she needed to make a good living so that she could pay bills by herself, because she and Daddy had separated. At this time Daddy continued to operate Bill's BBQ with a few family members and the rest went with Mama. Things started to get down to the wire for the opening and everything was good-to-go. The newspaper stands were stocked and the sidewalk was swept.

I will never forget the day that I had to type Mama's menu using one of those old Royal antique typewriters. The familiar clacking of the typewriter resulted from the keys striking the platen with force. I had to stand up to type because the

I tried to be friends with this thing in 1976.

typewriter sat on a stand. I thought my shoulders would never stop aching, and my feet got tired from standing so long. I tried my best not to make any mistakes—but I did. In order to get the menus typed in time for the restaurant to open, I used three sheets of typing paper, and inserted two sheets of black carbon paper between them. This allowed me to make three menus at a time. "Thank God for carbon paper!" Sometimes my fingers smudged the carbon; therefore, I held the edge of the paper with my fingertips. "Oh, No!" I hollered as my long fingers pressed down hard on a key sometimes touching the wrong one. The error was on the front page and it had created a domino-effect on the two carbon copies. It was a tough job, especially when I made a mistake. I had to remove the pages from the typewriter, remove the carbon, separate the pages, and then I tried to erase the mistakes with a pencil eraser. The task about drove me crazy!

Now I had to put the pages and carbon pages back together, insert them in the typewriter, and line them up precisely. If not, there were even more mistakes than before or I had to retype the entire page. By this time my head was hurting like hell! The thought of typing more pages made me more tired—especially using the carbon paper procedure with the possibility of making more mistakes—and made me a "nervous wreck." I was not about to tell Mama that I didn't want to finish because I knew she was depending on me. I typed the following.

Dip's Country Kitchen
Dinner Menu

$1/4$ Fried Chicken Dinners	$3.75
$1/4$ BBQ Chicken Dinners	$3.75
Chicken & Dumplings	$4.25
Vegetable Plate	$2.95

Then I typed the rest of the meals, listing the vegetables, and the breakfast items were typed on the back of the menu along with the drinks. Afterwards, I had to stuff the typed pages inside plastic menu sleeves. While inserting them the carbon pages smudged when they rubbed against the plastic. This was the most tedious job I had ever done! The more I typed the more frustrating the process was. I felt as if all the pressure was on me. If there were mistakes on the menu the customers would see them. I wanted the menus to be perfect. I had always been the creative one in our family, and that's why Mama chose me to create them. By the end of the week I had finished the menus and I was very happy camper.

Now that the menus were out of the way the only thing left to do was for Mama to go shopping for food. Fowler's food store was about three blocks down the street and around the corner from the restaurant. The store was a large grocery store with an old rustic look. There was absolutely nothing fancy about it. It was one of the first grocery stores in Chapel Hill, and it reminds me of Colonial Store where we shopped when I was a little girl. It sat right in the heart of downtown, catering to the walking crowd and the students at the university. Everyone loved to shop there because it was convenient and the employees seemed as if they had been working there since the store's beginning.

Fowler's was a perfect fit for Mama's business when she needed items fast. There was a butcher counter with glass fronted meat cases lined up against the back of the store. All the meats were on display with price signs pierced down inside so that customers could see the price per pound. Mama never asked us to purchase meat from the butcher counter. We knew that she wanted us to go to the section where the meats were prepackaged with prices, and then search for the price Mama had asked for.

On the first day the restaurant was open, Mama used a portion of the $64 she had to buy breakfast items and used the rest for change for her cash register startup. After that she couldn't buy food until she had made some money from prior meals. Breakfast allowed her to buy lunch and lunch bought dinner. Mama always let one of her children know when she needed items for the store. She'd say "Take ten dollars from the cash register and get cube steak for the lunch special and a dozen ears of fresh corn." When the child returned from the store, Mama immediately grabbed the bag of corn. I watched as she pulled the corn husk back with her long fingers and snapped off the top. She then twisted each ear of corn with both her hands to get rid of the silk, and rinsed the corn with cold water. Using a sharp knife, Mama trimmed the corn from its cob into an aluminum bowl then mixed it with lima beans that she had hulled the night before at home while watching TV. Every night we prepared some type of fresh vegetable. Sitting around we'd snap beans, shuck corn, and hull peas so they would be ready for the next day.

Back and forth down Rosemary Street my sisters and I went as fast as we could to restock the food supply for the next meal. After a few months, Mama was able to buy from a couple of the vendors that she had built a relationship with over many years at Bill's BBQ. The company's sales representatives knew from her past that Mama was a trustworthy business person—that's why they continued to do business with her with a small credit line until she increased her sales. Setting up her business turned out great because everybody from the landlord down to the vendors gave Mama a chance to prove herself—and she did.

August 25, 1976, Mama along with some of her children arrived at the restaurant at 7:00 am. Entering the dark building was somewhat a challenge as Mama cautiously searched to find her way to turn on the lights and all the equipment. A small pot of water for grits got the morning started. Chunks of potatoes lay on the hot grill, sizzling from the butter and sprinkled with chopped raw onions. After that, Mama grabbed an aluminum bowl and began to make biscuits, pouring in flour and adding shortening, while ordering some of us around to get her some buttermilk. "Fry bacon, sausage, and salmon cakes!" Constantly, she delegated jobs, while she continued to squeeze the sticky biscuit dough with her hands as she flipped the bowl over onto a floured table to knead. She cut her biscuits using an old empty baking powder can. Unfortunately, she found at the last minute that the oven did not work properly; however, Mama managed to bake a pan of biscuits to get the morning started. She didn't have money to repair the oven, but one thing I can say for sure is that Mama knew how to make do with what she had. After an hour, at 8:00 am, the restaurant doors were unlocked and Dip's Country Kitchen was now open for business, serving breakfast.

I was eagerly standing at the counter in front of the register as a customer, Jim Howerton, a student at UNC, came into the restaurant. I said, "Good morning, have a seat." I handed him one of our custom made menus. At this time, I wasn't concerned about whether or not the menu was good enough to present. I was just excited that a customer had walked through the door and wanted to order some of Mama's food.

When the customer noticed chicken and gravy on the menu, he said, "Chicken for breakfast!" "Try it, it's good." I said to him. "Then I'll have chicken and gravy," he said. He had never eaten chicken for breakfast. "How would you like your eggs?" "I would like one egg scrambled soft, hash browns and biscuits."

Then I asked, "Would you like jelly, honey, or molasses?" "Yes, I'd like molasses. This breakfast reminds me of how my grandmother cooked." "Would you like coffee, sir?" "Yes," he replied. I wrote the order down on a green numbered pad and immediately took it to the kitchen where Mama was standing in the kitchen waiting patiently for the first order. I placed the ticket inside the plastic mail holder that sat on the aluminum counter. Mama reached and grabbed the ticket and prepared the order. Jim loved his breakfast and said as he was walking out the door, "I'll be back!" One customer after the other trickled in to enjoy a great traditional style country breakfast. It didn't take long for the word to get around town that "Dip's" was the place to eat. Mama did not have money at this time to advertise. Word of mouth was and still is our most popular advertisement.

Making cornbread mix was the beginning of lunch preparation. Mama made cornbread batter everyday. She used her fingertips to scoop out shortening from the can, then rubbed her long fingers against the pan from top to bottom, greasing them so that the cornbread would not stick. Mama poured the batter in the pan, spread it out

Dip and Annette working the numbers

Dip, Lane, and Shawna

PHOTO BY TIFFANY PRATHER

evenly with a spatula, and wrapped a plastic bag around the top. Then she instructed me to carry the pan of cornbread batter to Bill's BBQ to bake in Daddy's oven while she held the door open for me. I carefully walked up the paved sidewalk holding on tight with both hands so that it would be just as Mama had poured it in the pan.

I made sure to keep the pan steady so that after it baked it would not be lopsided. This was Mama's special recipe and I certainly had to handle it with care. Soon the sidewalk came to an end, and I walked on the side of the street close to the curb and gutter up Rosemary Street and onto Graham Street. It was not a problem for Mama to bake her cornbread at Bill's BBQ. Even though she had separated from Daddy, our family bond was still there, and I felt like we were still a family. I had to wait for about ten minutes once the bread was done baking so that it could cool a little. Afterwards, I walked back down the street with the pan of hot cornbread with towels on both ends wrapped around my hands to protect them from the heat. The aroma from the bread was like an invisible cloud that made people stop along the sidewalk. When I passed them they realized that they smelled something delicious to eat. It was funny to me when I passed by people who smelled the aroma from the warm bread. I always turned around to look back to see what their expressions were, but I immediately turned back around because I knew that Mama was waiting. After I walked through the back door into the kitchen Mama was already holding a knife. I placed the pan of warm bread on the table where she had been eagerly waiting to cut it into slices to be served as part of the meals for the customers. While Mama was cutting cornbread, I wrote the daily special menu on a black dry erase board with a white marker that hung over the juke box at the entrance of the restaurant.

Today's Special
$3.75
Country Style Steak
Rice & Gravy
Limas & Corn
Cornbread or Rolls
Sweet iced tea
Pineapple Upside-Down Cake $1.25

Mama's desserts were a hit, especially her pecan pie. Most of the time Spring and I ate warm pecan pie with vanilla ice cream; however, Mama had to stop us from eating it so that she would have some to sell. She constantly reminded us that she was cooking the food for her customers to purchase and not for us to freely eat.

My family worked countless hours to help Mama so that she would not have to hire employees until she got her business off the ground. Many times I thought about how blessed Mama was to have her children help with her business. The family was the business and the complete staff at this time. Our life was what people called a "family affair," and that was just fine with us because they were indeed right.

Despite all the hard work and long hours my family made time for fun and family gatherings. Cooking was the one thing that all of my family members learned to do, but none of us was as good as Mama. Some of us wanted to make cooking a profession and some were just grateful for the opportunity to have learned the trade. My grandparents, Daddy, and Mama were all great cooks. My brothers, sisters, and I were trained by them. During holidays my family decided to start a cooking contest among the family members who wanted to participate, with Mama as the judge. All who wanted to come and join in on the taste test were welcome.

Bill started the contest with Easter being the occasion. His menu consisted of roasted Cornish game hens, broccoli with cheese sauce, wild rice and cheesecake topped with fresh strawberry sauce. His meal was delicious as the family sat around and ate until our bellies were about to burst. We discussed what thoughts Mama had about each dish so the rest of us would know what adjustments our meals needed to win. Mama's taste buds are that of an expert when it comes to traditional cooking. She was the definitely the one to ask.

The contest continued on the Fourth of July when we all went to Norma's house for an unforgettable cookout as her "contest meal." The entire family joined in on the fun. Norma was known for taking a few dollars and a bag of coupons to the grocery store to purchase enough food to make a feast for her family of six.

When I arrived at Norma's most of my family members were already there, along with her children. Her husband Thomas, nicknamed "Shortie," stepped out the kitchen door with a large pan filled of hand-molded hamburger patties. He was the "grill man" and his job was to cook the meats. The fish fryer was "kickin" out steam into Norma's face as she dropped chunks of cornmeal battered filet fish into the hot oil. When Shortie finished laying the burgers on the grill, he went over to the fryer and began to remove the cooked fish. Norma rushed back into the kitchen to make her delicious sweet hushpuppy recipe and then back outside to the fryer. The hot oil was loaded with scoops of hushpuppy mix floating around in the oil until they were browned to a crispy crunch. While waiting for dinner to be served everyone indulged in appetizers and cold sodas or beer from tubs of ice.

I decided to take a peek in the kitchen to see the action. "WOW!" Baked beans were bubbling as they were simmering on the stove top. I couldn't believe how much tossed salad Norma had prepared—it was sitting on her countertop along with the hotdog and hamburger condiments. Corn on the cob was wrapped in foil waiting for its spot on the grill. Norma's cookout took me back to the time when Mama was hosting our neighborhood cookouts that filled the air with an aroma of char-grilled food. Everybody enjoyed the cookout and we all decided that Norma was probably going to be the person to win the food contest. She cooked more like Mama than any of my brothers and sisters. Everyone could tell—even Mama.

Lane was the next cook with her Thanksgiving meal, and turkey was not cooked. Her meal included prime rib roast, fresh stewed white corn, fresh turnip greens seasoned with side meat, sourdough rolls, and banana pudding. This meal was right down Mama's line of eating more than my brother's Cornish hens. She was definitely going to tell us what she thought of our meals, good or bad. Mama grew up eating stewed corn for breakfast with biscuits and gravy. Her Papa "raised" fields of turnip greens every year. I wasn't sure whether I liked turnip greens yet, but the rib roast, corn and banana pudding were excellent.

Desserts have been my favorite since I was a child and continue to be what I love most. Throughout my teenage years, I often ate my dessert first since I missed out on a lot them when I was a young child. If I was going to leave something on my plate it was definitely not going to be dessert. The family contests came to an end when business required us to work more hours.

Council Family

Ed Cotten & Effie Edwards   William Minor & Mary Council

Mildred Cotten Council & Joe Council

CHILDREN

Norma Council Bell
Geary Wayne Council
Joe Nathan Council
William Thomas Council

Julia Council Smith
Sandra Elaine Council
Annette Marie Council
Anita Spring Council

GRANDCHILDREN

—NORMA—
Jonathan Neil Bell
Stefanie Michelle Bell
Sherry Renee Bell
Shawna Bell Atwater

—YEA-YEA—
Shaponica Taylash Council
Geary Wayne Council
Darius Wayne Horton

—JOE NATHAN—
Evan Farrington

—BILL—
Erika Council
Julian Council

—BON—
Panda Council
Tori Smith
Kim Smith

—LANE—
Cissy Council Green
Evan Council

—ANNETTE—
Millen Umoh

—ANITA—
Tonya Council

GREAT GRANDCHILDREN

Christian • Jessica • Imani • Andrew • Jaylyn
Natalie • Nicole • Monica • Ayanna • Shatia • Tashia
Breona • Brittney • Morgan • Erica • Victoria
Lauren • Jayln • Anderson

To add to our list of contests, Lane decided to accept a Bisquick cook-off contest invitation that the restaurant received in the mail. She spoke with Mama about what recipe they could create using some of the listed ingredients in the contest rules. Lane thought that the potato cake recipe that was used as a breakfast side special similar to hash browns would be perfect. The mashed potato based recipe was scooped out on a hot buttered skillet, and browned on both sides. Lane mailed the recipe along with the entry form to Bisquick Cook-off, and not much was thought about it after that.

Months later a representative from the contest called the restaurant to inform Mama that she won the recipe contest. An award was given along with a cash prize. For the first time the restaurant, along with the potato cake recipe, was featured nationally.

Sometimes being successful can cause you to make changes that are not anticipated. No matter how successful you are there will be bumps and sometimes bruises along the way. We found out that Mama could no longer use "country kitchen" together as part of her restaurant's name. In fact, another company had trademark rights to the combination phrase "country kitchen." Unfortunately, due to the national recognition, my family had to brainstorm on how we were going to figure out what Mama's new business name should be. We thought of "Dip's," but that wasn't quite enough. Then we thought, "We call her Mama, so lets put Mama in front of Dip's, and add Kitchen". "Mama Dip's Kitchen" was the new name and the trademark name was registered to protect the business from future legalities. We all thought that this was a better idea than "Country Kitchen." "That's it!" we all shouted. We didn't need to use the country kitchen phrase anyway,

*Changing
the name*

Mama was the chief cook of her restaurant and the name needed to reflect it. After that, business went on as usual.

Before we knew it, ten years of operation had passed, and "Mama Dip's Kitchen" was still a successful tiny restaurant. The time had come that we needed more space to accommodate more customers. Mama did not want to move from the downtown area. The only place that she could move her business was across town. "No!" Mama said. "I'll stay right where I am until something closer comes available. I don't want my customers that I have built a relationship with for all these years to have to find my restaurant if I move. Rosemary Street has been my landmark location since the beginning."

Next door to the restaurant was an antique furniture store. Later on they decided to move to a new location. My family was thrilled. Mama leased the space and hired a contractor to remodel. The restaurant did not have to close for the addition. The wall that separated the two businesses was the first thing torn down. New tiles were laid on the floor, paneling was attached to the walls. Mama purchased used booths, tables, and chairs, which added seventy seats to the previous twenty-two. Country lanterns were bought from the hardware store. They were attached to the walls above the booths along with pictures of old antique cars.

Now the restaurant had two front doors that entered into the building—an entrance and an exit. There was a brick wall that separated the bathrooms from the seating area. Plants were placed on the wall. Every day at work we watched each and every step of the process. Customers continued to come and soon lines began to form, especially at dinner. Large parties began to come and they waited patiently for a seat. New customers stated how they read local newspaper articles about Mama Dip's, and some brought news clippings to give to us as souvenirs.

As a result of this publicity, food critics learned about the restaurant. They came to the restaurant as "food spies." Some told our waiter who they were and others we figured out because of what they ordered. Their table would be filled with samplings of many of the menu items—much more than they could eat. The kitchen help also made a comment, "Only two people eating all this food?" Mama made sure all her employees paid attention to the customers. She sat in the kitchen at the end of the work table (her favorite spot), close to the dish machine so that she could make sure she saw plates that were not empty. It reminds me of when I was a young girl having to eat all my food. If more than a couple of bites of food was left on a plate, Mama felt that something was wrong. She wanted every customer to eat everything. By observing, she found out when recipes needed to be adjusted to make her food taste better.

Family members worked years of endless hours at Mama Dip's Kitchen. We became consumed with the business and running it. Mama hung in there and so did we. With all this working going on, we still found time to entertain our children. During the summer most of them harbored at Mama's house. Some came from other states and some were in town. Mama helped raised Spring's daughter, my niece, Tonya. At the time I was still in college and working at the restaurant in the evenings. Sometimes I stayed at the house with the grandkids during the day. The other members of my family dropped off their kids and headed to the restaurant until the shift changed, then I went to work to relieve someone else. Back and forth, we all took turns running the business and raising children.

I was glad when I went to work. It was quite a task sometimes trying to handle kids that were not mine, especially "hard head" (bad) kids. I tried to handle all situations on my own, but sometimes Mama had to be called to come immediately to calm things down. They were always fussing and fighting each other. There was hardly any peace in the house

Dip and Lane

Cousin Mike   PHOTOS BY TIFFANY PRATHER

after they ate breakfast. On one particular day, I had had enough of them misbehaving, and I called Mama to come see about her grandchildren. When the kids heard the rumble of her truck pulling up in the driveway all of them began to run for a seat to make it look as if they had been peaceful.

It was tough for Mama. She had already raised her own children. Now she wanted her grandchildren to enjoy each other's company at her home in the summer, but she also wanted peace. Mama's thunderous voice always quieted situations down. She entered the house through the side entrance as she began to holler each of their names. I went upstairs to my room and listened as I was having flashbacks of my childhood. She called them one by one, "Tonya, Geary, Nikki, Cissy, come here, and I mean right now!" They immediately knew that they were going to get the old fashioned "whuppin'," and therefore peace was again established. It didn't take long for Mama to calm down their attitudes and then she drove back to the restaurant to complete her work day. Mama often had to run the restaurant and her home at the same time. Taking care of both was alright with her since her rules governed all situations and everyone knew that.

Most of my family's meals were eaten at the restaurant because that's where we were most of the time. If it was a warm day I sat in my car to soak up some sun while I ate my meal. Some days the grandkids were driven to town to take a swim at the community pool where my brothers, sisters, and I learned how to swim when we were in elementary school. After swimming they walked to the restaurant in their wet swim suits and ashy bodies. We packed food to go, loaded them in the car, and hauled them back to Mama's house. They jumped out of the car even before I could turn the engine off—running as they seldom walked.

Mama's yard was like a park with a flower garden. There was a brick grill topped with racks from an old oven and picnic tables throughout the side and the back yard. After the kids grabbed a soda they raced back outside to take a seat at a picnic table where the food was spread out on the table. After they finished eating they continued to run around the yard as if they were a pack of horses, up and down the yard turning summersaults, screaming, and yelling with excitement. They enjoyed spending time at Mama's. This was their chance to be creative, have fun, and play games as my brothers, sisters, and I did when we were young children. In the evening when Mama pulled up in the driveway, they ran toward her truck screaming with excitement, "Grandma, Grandma ya' home!" They all began talking at the same time telling her how much fun they had that day, despite the whuppin' earlier. Mama has always said, "Children are children, let them be and remember that you were once a child, too."

Be a good steward.
Do what you
expect of others.

My Personal Venture

I continued to work at Dip's twenty hours a week, and I managed to save some money working there as a waitress. Even though I was back at home in Chapel Hill, and going to college in Durham, I wanted to move out on my own. I found an apartment in Carrboro and my roommate was a student at UNC. By this time I was not used to hearing Mama screaming my name to get up in the morning, and I was not ready to go back to the old way. My alarm clock was a pleasant change of pace.

I received a government grant that paid for the last three years of my college education. I was very excited, realizing that all I had to do was study, stay focused, and apply myself. I was certain that school was definitely my first priority. I didn't have to pay for tuition or my books—this was an opportunity to take a break from the busy scene at the restaurant. I felt that I needed some time off, especially on weekends. I could have more free time to socialize and add a sense of balance to my grueling schedule. Taking time off didn't last long because I was used to a paycheck. Even though I had money from my grant I was definitely a working girl—raised in a working family.

One day while I was sitting in the student union on campus, I overheard a couple of students' conversation about their jobs with the government. I approached them and asked if they could tell me more about the program. We talked every day, and for two weeks when I saw either one of them on campus, we discussed it again. Finally, I decided that I wanted to participate in the program. I applied for a part-time job during my school hours with the Environmental Protection Agency. The program offered employment that was geared toward assisting college students with the ability to earn a decent income while in college. This job was just right for me—it paid well, and I had always wanted to work in an office environment. The EPA was located on the seventh floor of the NC Mutual Insurance building in downtown Durham. My position was in the engineering department assisting the stenographer with clerical duties. I was happy about my new job and what I was learning about our environment and its standards for safety. I felt that there was a need for me to experience employment outside of the family business so that I could develop skills in other areas. When school was out for the holidays and during the summer, I worked full-time. I was eager about school and work, always striving hard at being the best person that I could be; however, I became burnt out.

During my sophomore year at NCCU, I became overwhelmed after continuously pushing myself into taking eighteen semester credits along with studying and working most of the time. I thought, "What a life...What a life!" By the end of my sophomore year, I thought a lot about taking a break from college, and everything else that was weighing me down. I simply needed time off, as my body, spirit, and emotional being needed rest.

During this time Bon had gotten married and she and her husband decided to move to Atlanta. Lane moved with them for a change of pace and for its metropolitan lifestyle, while the rest of the family was still working with Mama at the restaurant. They also wanted a more challenging opportunity instead of their every day routine back home. Having years of experience in the restaurant/retail field allowed both of them to find decent paying jobs. Bill's BBQ and Dip's had given them the training they needed. Bon and her husband accepted jobs at the Omni Hotel in downtown Atlanta, and Lane worked as an assistant manager at a bookstore at a mall in the suburbs.

My sisters were in Atlanta about nine months when I decided to join them. I was excited about getting what I thought was a new lease on life. When I arrived I immediately began to look for a job. It was not as easy as I thought it would be to find what I called a decent job with my two years of college behind me. After searching the job market for a while I decided to take a job at a fast-food Mexican restaurant across the street from where we lived. After working there for about two weeks I thought, "What in the world am I doing?" This was not my idea of employment, working in a restaurant; especially after I thought about how my two years college education should help me find something better. The type of restaurants that I grew up around were geared towards family traditions. Nevertheless, "How in the world was I going to be able to eat this stuff?" Mama had never cooked this type of food. I didn't understand why they mashed pinto beans as if they were white potatoes.

Mama prepared country cooking even if it was a hot dog or hamburger, and she made them the old fashioned way, molding her hamburger patties and preparing homemade chili for hotdogs. Mama's cooking was rooted down in my soul and that is all that I could think about at the time. I left Elizabeth City because it was not challenging and I missed Mama's cooking. Here I am again leaving a tradition that I was accustomed to because I needed a break. Nowhere in our family recipe was there a place for a break, but balance is the key to our survival.

I worked at the Mexican restaurant on the food assembly line that was fast paced, and I was efficient. My job was to stuff burritos, tacos, and tostados by tossing the ingredients on them as the next person scooped on the piping hot sauce. I will never forget one day, while I was working the line during the busy lunch rush, sauce that was intended to go on a burrito landed on the back of my hand. When I grabbed my wrist, I let out a painful moan, dropping to the floor curling my body into a squatting position. The hot sauce caused extreme pain that scorched my hand. Looking down at my hand reminded me of a raw piece of BBQ chicken ready to be baked. Once I gained my composure, I rushed to the employee hand sink, and ran cold water on my hand, rinsing off the sauce to soothe the pain.

The pain subsided somewhat with the cold water, and thinking back this was the first time that I had ever experienced being burnt this bad. The hot comb Mama used to straighten our hair when I was a growing up was nothing compared to this! The manager immediately set a first aid kit next to me, and I found burn ointment and gauze that I applied to my hand. After this mishap, I was done working for the day, and I went home. On my way as I walked home, I was thinking to myself, "Why am I putting myself through this?" The fast food experience was not at all what I had anticipated. About a month later I quit working there. I wanted to work where it would be enjoyable. I decided to experience a job in modeling part-time before I returned back home to finish my studies in accounting.

The weekend had come when Joe and one of his friends flew down from Louisville to Atlanta to visit. It was around nine o'clock on Saturday night when we were all sitting around in the living room watching a movie. We were startled when we heard an explosion from outside. We noticed the windows in the front of our apartment were shattered and the electricity immediately shut off. We jumped up, rushing to the front door. Lane opened it, and we all crowded behind her trying to take a peek. "Oh my God!" she said. I turned around and briskly headed toward the back door while the others stood for a moment to look on. I was preparing to take cover if needed, while they stood there and looked as long as they liked—I was out of there! There had been a head on collision in the middle of the busy four lane road. The accident involved a compact car and a gasoline tanker truck, the kind that delivers gasoline to convenience stores. The car was pinned underneath the truck. The explosion created a ball of fire that was so huge and powerful that it broke out all the windows in the apartment buildings halfway through the complex—we lived in a large apartment complex. Our apartment was close to the front entrance near the road where the accident happened. The fire and police personnel were already on the scene, using their megaphones to advise everybody to evacuate their apartments immediately, and move to the very back of the complex. I was already standing outside the back door when the rest of my household decided to exit following my path. Once everybody in our house was outside there was another explosion with illumination that lit up the entire area from the flames of the burning fuel.

The emergency personnel began to run away from the scene, so we knew that we were in a dangerous situation. The only light outside was from the flames. While I was running, I stumbled into a ditch and found myself trying to recover from a "belly buster" on the ground. I was desperate to get out of the way, as my thoughts led me to believe that there was a possibility of being blown into bits and pieces. I was petrified, and all I knew was that I was going to get the hell out of harm's way and as far as I could back into the complex for my safety. My brother and sisters laughed at me until they cried. They said I resembled a cowboy scrambling to get off the ground after falling off a bull. Growing up, I was always called a "scaredy cat."

Several hours later into the night we were allowed to go back into our apartment, but the flames were still burning strong. We cautiously walked back up to the front of the complex, finally getting a glimpse of the car that was pinned underneath the tanker. The car had burned to a crisp and it appeared that the tanker was going to also. The next morning when we got out of bed we immediately went to look out the window to see if the tanker was still burning, and it was. It did not matter what was still going on outside—this was a work day and everyone had to shower without electricity and possibly without hot water. This day was no different from any other as I continued to look for a job. Lane, Bon, and her husband went to work—Joe and his friend left for the airport going back to Louisville.

Lane met a friend in our neighborhood from New York that constantly talked to her about our similar interest in modeling. We had previously arranged to go to downtown Atlanta on Monday morning to meet a photographer to pose for our modeling portfolio. When I arrived at her apartment about three buildings back into the complex she was just walking out of her door. We quickly walked back to the front of the complex to catch the early bus to downtown. As we approached the road the city bus was already there loading people on. "Oh no!" both of us said at the same time, "We're gonna miss the bus!" The traffic was heavy on both sides of the road. Once we had reached the edge of the sidewalk cars stopped to let us cross as they saw us waving at the bus driver to wait for us.

When we approached the middle of the forty-five miles per hour speed limit road, a driver trying to get around the cars that had stopped for us traveling at fifty miles per hour hit me. The impact tossed me to the other side of the road into oncoming traffic. Many years have passed, but I still think to myself how blessed I am. I thank God that the traffic on the other side of road in both lanes where my body landed had already stopped for us to cross. I remember crawling using my elbows to get out the road and onto the curb. This accident happened suddenly, and I had no idea that I was struck by a car, until I noticed blood on my clothes. I could feel my mouth and right leg had begun to swell. The repairmen from the electric company were still repairing electricity to the area where the tanker accident happened a few days ago. Firemen were still at the scene also. Everyone in the immediate area witnessed my accident. The firemen immediately called for emergency medical service. Even though I was injured I knew that I was going to be okay.

When the emergency personnel arrived at the scene they began to assist me. I was in shock, and all I could think about was getting up and walking away. They had to ask me over and over to settle down and not move while I was examined, and if my body hurt anywhere. "No, I don't feel pain." The EMS cut my jeans starting from my ankle up to my thigh. I reached down and touched my swollen right leg. They wanted to take me to the hospital, which meant riding in the ambulance. I pleaded with them, "Please don't make me ride in that ambulance—pleeeeeeeease!" All I could think about was when I was a little girl and the red ambulance responded to an emergency call. I feared ambulances because back then the ambulance and hearse sat side by side in the driveway next door to my grandparents' house. I associated the ambulance ride with death, because often the hearse pulled out shortly afterwards.

When the accident happened Bon was on her way to work, sitting at the stop sign, waiting to pull out onto the road. She saw me get hit by the car. From the look on her face when she approached me on the curb, I could see that fear had set in. She did not know how bad I was hurt but I knew she must have been thinking the worst. After I begged and told the EMS staff that I was going to be fine, they allowed Bon to drive me to the hospital emergency. They radioed my arrival ahead, and a team of doctors and nurses were waiting for me when we got there. They began to examine me, telling me that no one coming to the hospital had ever survived being struck by a vehicle going forty-five mph. My face had swollen more and a tooth had been knocked out, but I did not have any head injuries.

My knee was another story. The accident caused torn ligaments around my knee. At this time the doctor put a cast on my leg that went from my hip down to my toes on my leg. This accident happened in the middle of summer. The doctor wasn't sure if I needed surgery at the time and wanted to see what my leg looked like the next day.

Bon took me home with crutches, and a wheelchair was to be delivered to our apartment the next day. When we arrived at home from the hospital, getting out of the car was difficult. I really had to concentrate moving around with the full leg cast. It was a tough twenty-four hours until I went to the specialist for the evaluation the next day.

I received good news and bad news from the specialist. First, he took the cast off, but I knew it wouldn't be off for long. He examined my leg and the good news was that I didn't need surgery. The bad news was that he had to drain fluid from behind my kneecap, and that meant a needle. I did not have Mama's skirt to hang onto this time as I did as a child getting "shots." I just closed my eyes, gritted my teeth as I frowned while the needle penetrated my skin to my bone. I will never forget it hurt like hell! When the doctor was done, all I could say was, "Thank you, Jesus!" A new cast was put on my leg. The doctor told me that I would have to wear the cast for three more months. All I could think about was, "How the hell am I going to do this?" But I didn't have a choice.

My family had been notified back home in North Carolina. Mama was waiting for me at our apartment when Bon and I returned home from the doctor's. Once she knew for herself that I was okay and that I could manage, she returned to Chapel Hill, as she was busy operating her restaurant.

The next few months were a challenge. With my leg in a cast, along with a wheelchair, I had to make my way around the house and outside for fresh air. One day I managed to wheel myself out the front door onto the sidewalk. I was happy that I finally made it outside. My sisters had left for work early that morning, and I had the pleasure of staying home alone. I was just fine, and I managed to entertain myself for about eight hours until someone returned home.

Once during my recuperation I pushed the wheels forward on my new set of legs (wheelchair) and headed toward the rear of the complex. My accident happened in the summer and the children in the neighborhood were out of school. They came to my rescue when they saw me struggling to get over a speed bump. About four of them came running as fast as they could to help me. When they got closer to me all I could think about was when Mama's grandchildren came to visit in the summer—all playing together most of the day. I became childlike despite my adult status. These kids were my new-found friends and the drivers of my wheelchair for the rest of the summer. They were excited and took turns pushing me up and down the complex and sometimes to their house, where I became friends with their parents. I will never forget those children—they "made my days."

Often I became bored sitting around the house so I decided to move back to Chapel Hill even though my leg was not completely healed. It took another three months for my leg to heal, and after that I was ready to work. My siblings and I were blessed that we were always welcomed back to work at Mama Dip's Kitchen. Mama looked forward to any of us returning, since she knew that we were experienced. I returned to college to finish my degree in accounting the next semester.

Mama's business had really taken off, and she had hired employees that were not family. I watched as Mama rolled her biscuits out on the table, while coaching an employee on how to fry an egg. She always paid attention to the dishwasher and mainly the person making her recipes, "Make sure you stir that good. The flavor is what makes it special," she'd say.

She was the same Mama—some things just don't change. Reflecting back, Atlanta was the place that I had experienced the most drama. First, I burned my hand, then the tanker truck accident that could have killed all of us, and I will never forget getting hit by a car.

I was glad to be home! After my Atlanta experience I really understood how important it was to finish my college education.

Bumps and bruises are OK. Heal and move forward.

Another Get-Away to DC

It seemed like my last two years of college were just a few months and it was over and done with. I graduated in 1981 at the end of the summer school session. I didn't attend my graduation ceremony. Looking back on those days I wish I had, but at the time I was just ready to move on. By this time I had grown into a strong-willed individual in search of new opportunities, which led me to moving to Washington, DC. Yea-Yea had lived there for several years before moving back to Chapel Hill. While in DC he befriended the Gallmon family, who reminded him of our family. When my brother found out that I wanted to move there, he introduced them to me. It seemed awkward that I met them over the phone. They were very nice, inviting me to stay at their home until I could find a job and my own place to live. I was grateful to have met them and claimed them as my family away from home.

Before moving to DC I lived with my Grandma and Daddy. Grandma didn't like to be by herself. Grandpa had passed away from heart failure. The "Merchant Man" that fried the best chicken in Chapel Hill was gone. Norma and her husband were operating Bill's BBQ.

None of my family members thought that I would leave Chapel Hill. My college years were over—I was at a point in my life where I needed to be independent since the "real world" was waiting. Even though I wanted to move, I was nervous about it. If I was going to accomplish my goals, I knew that I had to step out on faith—and why not, since this was a good opportunity to apply my hard-earned education?

The day before I left, I packed my car with all my belongings. I studied the driving directions that Yea-Yea and the Gallmons had given me. I woke up early on a Saturday morning and started driving north toward Virginia. I managed to find my way heading straight up Interstate 95 until finally after five hours I was sitting in traffic on the Fourteenth Street Bridge.

"Wow!" I thought. The last time I visited Washington was when I was a Girl Scout. I looked to the right and there was the Potomac River, and nearby was the Washington International Airport. The airplanes looked as if they were going to land right above my head. I held onto my directions—now I really had to pay attention to where I was going. Then I looked to the left and there stood the Washington Monument, taller than any other building. After crossing the bridge, I was downtown at 14th and K Streets. While sitting at the traffic lights I watched the crowds of people walking back and forth across the street —ladies dressed in business suits and sneakers, couriers on bikes with backpacks attached to both sides. I was almost at my destination, but I wasn't sure which way to go, so I stopped to use a pay phone to call my friends. While speaking with them I made sure that I was observant, paying close attention to my surroundings. Sure enough, I was not far from their house.

I was directed which way I should go and I hurried back to my car. After five more minutes of driving there was C Street. As I approached the "row houses" I began to slow down. I reached over to roll down the passenger side window so that I could see the house numbers. I pulled up to a line of "row houses" and all of them seemed to have the same number—1606. I pulled my car to the curb and parked. The closer I walked toward the houses, the clearer the numbers became. I walked up the steep steps that were consistent to every house in the neighborhood. I rang the doorbell and was able to see inside through the glass storm door. I saw a lady walking toward the door, and immediately she knew who I was. "You must be Neecy" she said. "Yes ma'am." I said. "Come on in," she said as she called her daughter, Diane, announcing that I had arrived.

I was happy that I had finally arrived at my destination since I felt somewhat nervous traveling alone. After we sat around the living room for about an hour getting to know one another, I was now feeling the "neighborhood bonding" with my new family, even though I was just beginning to know them. Afterwards, I decided to get my belongings out of the car. When I got back to the house, Diane was standing on the porch to tell me that I would be staying at her house next door. She was Yea-Yea's friend that he introduced to me over the phone. The Gallmons seemed to be a close knit family and reminded me of my family. The only difference that I saw was that we would never live side by side. We had worked side by side for many years and some members of my family continue to do so, but living next door would be out of the question. I admired the Gallmons for being close.

After getting settled over the weekend, job hunting was the first thing on my agenda. Diane told me that her family would do whatever they could to help me out. I thanked them over and over for being there for me. They welcomed me into their home even though they had never seen my face. "What an honor," I thought, as I immediately felt that I was about to build a lifetime relationship. Monday morning I was awakened by the sound of cars and city bus engines roaring as they drove back and forth outside my bedroom window. Because of this I never used my alarm clock—the noise woke me. There weren't any birds chirping, just the hustle and bustle of city life. Diane, her sister Shirley, and I got dressed and dashed out the door to catch the bus. While we boarded the bus, I thought to myself, "Why in the world are we riding the bus when their cars are parked in the drive-way?" Riding the bus and subway was their way of traveling during the weekday, unless they were going to Maryland or Virginia. On weekends they drove. I wasn't quite sure if I was going to get used to their system of transportation.

We rode the bus about eight blocks when it came to an immediate stop. Unprepared, I almost toppled over. I watched them hustle off the bus leaving me behind as they began to run. They turned around and yelled, "Run, we don't want to miss the train!" I thought to myself, "This is crazy, why we are running for a train when we can wait for the next one?" Anyway, I had to run and catch up with them. Upon entering the subway station we had to go down what looked like about a hundred steps underground to where we were to catch a train. Before we were completely down to the bottom of the steps we could hear the trains approaching.

While we stood in the midst of the crowd and waited for the next train to come, I heard the sound of footsteps stomp-ing on the pavement. I looked around to see people running towards us. I thought "What is going on?" At the sound of the forthcoming trains, people began to run so that they could get on before it was too crowded. We rode the train through about three stations and then we got off near the government building where my friends worked. Diane and Shirley showed me where I needed to go to fill out an application for government employment.

I was hired about a month later on a temporary assignment working for the federal government's Department of Defense. I was working with the Procurement Department for the United States Army. I used to wonder what people in the military did all day. Well, I found out that the military personnel worked just the same as civilians. I enjoyed working with the defense department and my job as a procurement clerk, where I met more friends that showed me how to get around other areas of DC.

Educating myself with DC seemed a bit much when it came to driving my car. Riding the bus was my guide to learning streets and points of interest around the city. I watched closely as the driver turned onto streets and avenues at every intersection. I always sat close to the front so that I could ask questions. I rode the bus for about a week until I learned the route to use for driving. Diane and her sister thought that I was out of my mind, but I was determined to drive in DC. Down south we drove our cars and I simply wasn't accustomed to rapid transit and having to "haul ass" to catch those buses and trains. I wanted to have the ability to go directly to my car after work and drive myself rather than waiting for public transit.

There was one other thing about the subway stations and bus stops that bothered me—there were always homeless people hanging out. It really made me nervous; I removed myself from the environment by driving so that I would have peace of mind while I traveled throughout the city. I felt more secure in my car, even though I had to listen to the radio announcing the missing persons listing every hour during the day. I couldn't believe the number of people missing in just one city. The fast pace of DC was not like home in Chapel Hill where things moved much slower and there definitely wasn't a missing persons list. As time went by I became more comfortable with my surroundings, since I had learned DC and the surrounding areas. However, I knew that I didn't want to stay in DC forever—this experience in my life was just another stepping stone.

A few months after I arrived in Washington I received a call from Mama telling me about a cousin who lived in the area. She told me that she had met him at a family reunion a couple of weeks prior. Mama made sure she knew all of her "kin folks," even if they were distant relatives. She enjoyed going to family reunions. She would always tell her children, "Know your family so that your children will also know." I wrote down their phone number and was excited about calling them. Their names were Jim and Catherine Couch.

I did not know how far down our family tree I had to go to find this family's connection to Mama. I didn't know their age or anything that I could use to familiarize myself with them. The next day I telephoned them and a gentleman answered the phone, "Hello." The sound of his voice was that of a smart, intellectual, proper-speaking gentleman with a distinct northern accent. I could feel his confidence through the phone. I honestly thought that I was calling a distant relative who'd be a "country bumpkin." Boy, was I wrong!

After I spoke with Jim for a few minutes, he invited me to his home to meet his family. While writing down directions to his house all I could think about was the time I was lost for over an hour, driving around and around, stuck on the north-west side of the city. Apparently, I had no sense of direction, but generally, I could remember streets. I was not sure about driving over to his house since I was still learning the area. My destination read 49 U St. NW. Jim described his neighborhood with small and narrow streets—I had to drive slowly up to his house since cars were parked along both sides of the street. I found his house next to the fire hydrant as he stated. I parked and got out of my car and looked up and down the street to observe the neighborhood. I noticed that the "row houses" were a little different from where I was living at the time on the northeast side of the city. In this neighborhood houses were very close to the street with hardly any yard.

I walked toward their house, reached and grabbed the wrought iron gate that led to four narrow steps up to the front door. The door was open, but the storm door was latched. I rang the doorbell as I glimpsed inside. A short dark-skinned man approached the door, "Come in my dear, I am your cousin, Jim. Come on back and meet my wife." I followed him through the house toward the kitchen and noticed their fine antique furnishings. Jim introduced me to his lovely wife, Catherine. "She is the light of my life," he said. How nice that sounded as I had never been exposed to this type of affection, just the love of hard work. Daddy and Mama rarely displayed this type of closeness toward each other. The Couches truly loved each other, and I thought, "What a way to introduce the one you love." Jim told me that they had been married for sixty-five years and she was still his sweetheart—he was a proud husband.

His wife was cooking dinner when I arrived and she invited me to join them. I enjoyed a delicious meal that she served on her fine china. Entertaining was special to her. If I hadn't known better I would have thought Mama was in the kitchen. After dinner we talked for a while about our family history and how Jim was related to my family. Afterwards, I was eager to return home before dark so that I could find my way back. Jim and Catherine invited me to come and visit anytime.

I grew very close to them, visiting often, and attending church with them on Sundays. On one occasion, Jim drove me to Capitol Hill as he felt that it was important for me to meet a state representative for North Carolina. At the time I was still seeking permanent employment and obtained a letter of recommendation from this office. As a result of this, I obtained permanent employment with ARC (Association for Retarded Citizens) in Falls Church, Virginia. I learned from Jim how important it is to know your government and its state affiliation.

I especially enjoyed Catherine as we often enjoyed cooking and baking together. I baked several of Mama's delicious carrot cakes, making the cream cheese frosting in different colors. When the cakes were sliced they looked beautiful on her fine dessert dishes. Catherine took many of the cakes to church to share with members on special occasions and also to homeless people who came to their church to be fed everyday. I felt that cooking and baking for others was my opportunity once again to give back to the community as I had learned growing up.

I lived in Washington, DC for three years. While I was there I married and had a child. Soon after, I decided that the city was not the place I wanted to raise my daughter.

Build relationships.
You will need them
down the road.

Raising My Daughter, Millen

Two years later, divorced and with my precious baby girl Millen (pronounced M'Lynn), I moved back to Chapel Hill. Millen's name was derived from her maternal grandmother's name, Mildred—"Mil" and her paternal grandmother's name, Helen—"Len." Her middle name is Neecy, my nickname.

We lived with Mama for a while. After six months I decided that we needed our own space and rented a townhouse for us. The challenge of being a single mom was about to become a reality, and I wanted to make sure Millen had the best guidance. I enrolled her in daycare—she had spent the first year and a half of her life with me every day—and daycare was a new environment for her. Millen was an anxious little girl. She seemed a bit timid, but eager to learn how to read.

When Millen was three and a half years old she cried because she did not know how to read. I read book after book with her until she learned. At the age of four she could read any book on a first grade level. It was important to me that my daughter mastered the basics of education.

When I was growing up my parents did not use proper English, but I thought what they were saying was correct. I missed multiple choice spelling words on tests in elementary school because the answer I circled was how my parents pronounced them. I made sure that every word in my sentences was spoken correctly to Millen. I never said "Yeah." I said "Yes." I never said "Naw." I said "No."

The time came quickly for Millen to enroll in elementary school. She attended Seawell Elementary, which was named after a long-retired teacher that I remembered from when schools were integrated. The morning I drove Millen to school for kindergarten, I cried. My daughter was growing up. She was eager with her slightly empty book bag hanging across her shoulders. I held her hand tight while we walked to her class. Millen walked with her shoulders erect and her body poised. She was excited about school and told me, "I'm going to do well in school."

When it was time to study for her spelling test, she sat across from me at our dining table. I called out each word aloud. Millen spelled each word aloud as I read them, going down the list. Pronouncing each word slowly for Millen, I said to her, "Spell cooomme." She slowly recited one letter at a time, "C...O...M...E." "Spell beee-hiiinnd." again she spelled the word, "B...E...H...I...N...D." I could hear in her voice when she was confident or apprehensive. One after the other I called out Millen's spelling words. I did not tell her which words she spelled incorrectly until the last word was called out. After that, I again called out only the words that she had misspelled.

Then I'd have her take a written test. I checked her test as if it was a real classroom test. Any words that were still misspelled I called them over again until she got all the words correct. Lastly, I gave her the test again with all the words. As a result, Millen always received one hundred on spelling tests. Because of her excellence in reading and spelling she wrote a book called, "The Pictionary." Her book is a self-made dictionary with words and illustrated pictures representing each letter from A to Z.

Millen consistently mastered each grade level; by the time she reached fifth grade she no longer needed my assistance with her school work. She continued to be an honor student. I wished that I had constant help with my school work when I was growing up. Because of work, Mama didn't have time to help my brothers, sisters, and me study—we depended on each other.

Most days after school our kids came to "Dip's." Millen along with my niece, Cissy, spent many evenings there doing homework. Millen loved her grandmother's BBQ and often asked for a sandwich. After she had eaten her sandwich, she was ready to go. It didn't take long for our kids to get tired of coming and sitting at the restaurant. Millen often told me, "I want to go home, take me home," but I could not leave her at home alone, she was too young.

Sometimes after school I would drop her off at the public library. It was her favorite place to go—she did homework and signed books out. I escorted Millen inside the library to help her get settled, and then I'd tell the staff that I was going to leave her. Millen loved to read and won numerous contests at school for reading the most books in a school year. About an hour later, I arrived back to pick her up, and she would be sitting quietly at a table with a stack of books. I gave her our library card and watched her with an armful of books as she proceeded to the counter to check them out.

I signed Millen up to join the Pines of Carolina Girl Scouts. She became a Brownie along with some of her friends who lived in our neighborhood. Millen was friendly and had a lot of friends. I participated in Brownie Scouts when it was time to sell cookies; we sold them to family and the employees at the restaurant. She also sold cookies to regular customers. Because of work, I didn't have time to go around town and sell cookies throughout the neighborhoods. Millen was very successful selling cookies at the restaurant. Her second year as a Brownie she won the contest for selling the most boxes of cookies. Two hundred boxes were sold to restaurant traffic.

I continued to keep Millen busy when she was a young girl. I didn't want her to have too much idle time. She loved all activities and was well liked in middle school. Millen played the clarinet, just as my brother Bill had. She was a cheerleader and a member of the school's track team. She ran as hard and as fast as she could, leaping over each hurdle, while I stood in the crowd of parents to cheer her on. I was proud of Millen. She never won a race, but she mastered jumping over hurdles, and that was good enough for me. One day I asked her, "How do you like running track?" She replied, "It's okay Ma, I'm doing it for you." "Oh, nononononono, absolutely not! If you are not doing it for Millen, then don't do it," I replied. At the end of track season Millen decided that she no longer wanted to run track. I was happy with her for being able to make this decision on her own.

Parents often pressure their children to do what makes the parents happy. As I reflect back, my brothers, sisters, and I had to sing in the choir at church even though we couldn't carry a tune to make Mama happy. As teenagers we were forced to work—by this time we had to buy our own clothes even if we didn't want to. Once we were forced, we became attached and found ourselves living our grandparents', Daddy's and Mama's dream. We could have walked away. I stayed because I felt that I owed it to my brothers and sisters to tough the legacy out. We were there in the beginning and I felt that we had earned our right to stay to the end. There's no way in the world I would ever allow my daughter to live my dream. It's important for everyone to live their own dream. Millen is the light of my life and my best friend.

In high school, Millen continued to be an honor student. I was busy working at my local government town job and at Mama Dip's Kitchen. Millen started to experience difficulties and became frustrated with life in general along with "teenage melodrama." She started missing days at school. I worked about twenty five miles away from our home and had no idea she was missing school. She forged my signature on the absentee forms that she was given and erased phone messages from our answering machine that were left for me from her school. Millen missed fifty-one days of school in her junior year, and the school year was far from the end. I was devastated when I found out from the school counselor.

I received a letter from Millen's school that they needed to meet with both of us to discuss her absences. Her six teachers, the guidance counselor, Millen, and I sat around a wooden table. Each of the teachers gave their view on the status of my daughter in their classroom. I sat back in my chair and listened in total shock as I noticed the somber look on her face. She knew that she was breaking my heart with her behavior concerning school.

I listened to the teachers speak about how talented she was. Each of them read her grades, with zero's being dominant. I sobbed uncontrollably. Millen began to cry as she looked across the table at me and said, "I'm sorry, Ma, but I don't want to go to school any more." She had given up. Millen earned B's without even trying. "Where did I go wrong? My daughter no longer wanted to attend school. How could this be happening to me?" I constantly questioned myself.

I had quite a few meetings at the school to get to the root of her problem. I felt like the final meeting ended with the counselor suggesting that I basically needed to throw my hands up. I continued to come to the school to assist with Millen's situation and I continued to express my concerns. I was one of the few parents that built relationships with my child's teachers and guidance counselor. This was my child and her education was at stake—I was not about to turn her over to the world haphazardly. The guidance counselor advised me to go home and go on with my life, "You have done all you can do," she told me. But I knew that I had not done enough—my child was not going to be a statistic! I drove back home with my bloodshot eyes and an ashy face from the dried tears.

After I pulled the car into the driveway, I sat for a few minutes taking deep breaths before getting out of the car. My mind was racing; I wasn't giving up on Millen. More than ever, she needed me and I was determined to do everything in my power to help her. The mission was on! With my long legs, it only took four long leaps for me to get to the top of my staircase to my bedroom.

First, I felt that Millen's father needed to be made aware of her situation. I phoned him in Texas where he was living and explained to him what was going on and that I was reaching out to him for support. He asked to speak to her. When Millen got on the phone he demeaned her, told her that she never would be anything and gave her a tongue lashing. If I had any idea that he would react this way I would never have made the phone call. I would have never attempted to seek his input or help. My daughter needed more emotional support now more than ever! The phone call devastated Millen and my heart went out to her. I immediately wrote him a letter expressing that I would not allow him to tear down what I had built since Millen was two years old being a single parent. He seldom contacted her since we were divorced; now his communication wasn't necessary, needed or wanted.

I now realized that the school couldn't help us, her daddy didn't want to help us, and as always "the ball was in my court." I needed to take control and run with it. My brain was going a mile a minute as my body trembled. I needed to move fast for Millen's sake.

It was a normal school day for most students except for Millen. I will never forget that dreadful morning. I woke up to the beeping sound of the alarm clock as it vibrated on the dresser across the room. Going to work was out of the question; it was not a normal day for me either. Taking a bath and brushing my teeth didn't seem necessary. It was a quiet morning. I refused to turn on the TV or the radio—I needed time to meditate. I lay in my bed, hugging the comforter to my chin in a fetal position. I had sobbed throughout the night. My pillow was soaked with tears. I sat up to flip my pillow over to the other side as I propped the pillows up against the head board. I stared out my bedroom window, watching as the cars passed by.

"This is a new day," I thought. "I have done all that I know to convince Millen to stay in school. All I can do now is to relax." I tried to prepare myself by being calm; I listened as the sound of water was running in her bathroom. A few minutes later I heard her footsteps as she walked into my bedroom. She stood in the middle of the floor refusing to come close, and said "Ma, I'm going to return my books to school now." "Okay," I said. It wasn't okay, it was out of control. North Carolina laws states that a child can quit school at age sixteen. I was angry and wanted to know who these law makers were. I had no idea at the time that there was a law to protect a sixteen-year-old who wanted to quit school. I cried every day when I found out there was a law to protect her. I wasn't so mad with my daughter—I was mad with the State of North Carolina.

I listened as the rumbling sound of her car backed out of the driveway. I began to pray aloud and I said to God, "I have no more tears to shed; it seems that Millen has made up her mind to quit school. I have been the best mother that I know how. If you allow this to happen to us then you must have something better in store for me and Millen. I put all my trust in your judgment so that we can move forward to the next stage."

Millen had been gone for quite some time. I thought to myself, "What is she doing?" when the phone rang. It was the counselor from the school. "This is the school calling to let you know we still have Millen here. She is determined to quit school. We have not given up, just wanted to touch base with you about her progress." About an hour later I heard the sound of a car coming down our cul-de-sac. I peeked through the blinds from my bedroom window—it was Millen. She came straight upstairs, plopped down on my bed, threw a piece of paper at me and said, "Here is my new schedule." I shouted, "Thank you, Jesus!!!!! I knew that you would see us through this." Millen explained that she decided to stay in school because the counselor made her a schedule that she could not turn down. Now she was in school half a day with more hours to work to make money, as she wanted to do.

I got myself together after not getting any sleep the night before. My brain would not and could not stop trying to figure a way to help my daughter. I knew in my heart that something else could be done. I knew that there had to be answers. Exhausted, I got out of bed, got my purse and started to shuffle through everything to find my health insurance card. I called my carrier to find out the status of my policy relating to counseling sessions. Millen and I both were covered. I flipped through the pages of the phone book to find a psychologist, and I immediately called to arrange an appointment for Millen.

Millen and I went to her appointment. After a thirty minute session, my daughter was diagnosed as being clinically depressed. "Okay," I thought to myself, "Now what?" The doctor told me that she needed a prescription for an antidepressant. I was again devastated because while growing up Mama taught my brothers, sisters, and me to be mentally tough. That's all I knew, that was Prozac to us. I had to sign papers for Millen to take this medication. I pondered for about fifteen minutes and decided to agree with the doctor. It seemed to have taken every muscle in my body to make myself do this. But it was necessary and in her best interest. The counseling sessions were frequent, but they helped solve her problem. It took less than a year for the transformation.

The following week Millen was assigned to work out of a computer lab. After discussion the school officials and I agreed that it would be in Millen's best interest to be separated from other students in order to eliminate distractions. She went to school later than regular students and left earlier. Everything went well and Millen was back on track with school. She was able to complete everything she missed in six weeks. I knew she could do it. It was in her from the beginning. She managed to complete the 11th grade—for the first time in her life without honors. Millen was determined to do her very best her senior year, as being an excellent student was her forté. Her senior year went very well. She worked as hard as she could to do better since she wanted to go to college. At this point, I was only thinking of getting her through high school.

Raising my daughter through her teenage years was a constant struggle for me. After putting my faith in God things began to change. One evening when I was sitting in my family room watching television, I heard the door bell ring. "Who could that be?" I thought and sat for a few more seconds before I went to open the door. There were two ladies and one gentleman. They introduced themselves and the church that they were representing. I closed my eyes for a second, took a deep breathe, looked up at the sky, and said, "Thank you God for sending your Shepherds, come in." They knew from the expression on my face that I needed whatever it was they had to present.

I immediately turned the television off and they began to discuss salvation. I was raised in church and I was a member of a church at this time. I felt like there was something missing in my life that was causing me not to understand my struggles. It seemed to me that I needed to understand more clearly life's process according to the Bible. They began to discuss Jesus Christ and his purpose for our lives. They also discussed enjoying the fruits of the spirit. I gave my life to Jesus Christ and he saved me on this day. I was happy that the second time the group came back my daughter was also saved. It amazes me how God had allowed this to happen in our life at this crucial time. As I now reflect back on my life I am able to understand the process God has for me each day as I continue to grow as a Christian.

Millen graduated from high school in June, 2000. I had a chance to attend her graduation ceremony after all. I thought that I would cry the entire time, but I managed to keep a dry face.

Millen was accepted to North Carolina Central University where I am an alumna. I was excited about Millen attending a historically black university where I thought her educational excellence would be noticed. She decided after her freshman year to major in biology. Millen wanted to be a dentist. While studying biology, Millen decided that it was not what she wanted to do, and she was only pursuing it for the potential income. However, after exploring her options during her sophomore year, she found that psychology should be her major, as she completely identified with this profession. Because of Millen's high school experience she felt that this was a profession in which she could help others who struggled with life's difficulties. Millen also felt that the passion she had in this area was something that she could give to the community free of charge.

Millen was mastering her major, psychology. Her professor and advisor offered her a Marc Scholarship. Marc Scholarships are offered to students that are committed to enrolling in graduate school in biomedical sciences. A student must maintain a GPA of 3.0 or better in his/her major. The Scholarship is limited to under-represented minority students who are African-American, Hispanic-American, Native-American, or native to the U.S. Pacific Islands. The benefits of the scholarship include full tuition, summer research internships, mentoring by the MARC Faculty, and support during the application process to graduate school. She had not applied for this scholarship, nor did she know about it. But it was okay with Millen as she was going to attend school free her senior year. "I feel like I have won the lottery," she said to me. "When you prepare yourself, the opportunity will come, and it will find you," I said to Millen.

I now had a second chance to attend a graduation ceremony.

Millen graduated from college with honors in May 2004. She now is a graduate student at Pepperdine University in Malibu, California. I am ecstatic and proud that I am going to have an opportunity to attend a third graduation!

I can now say that I knew I had been the best mother that I could be. The basic educational foundations that I taught my daughter were instilled in her even when she got off track in high school. No matter how crazy kids can get, they never forget the values that are instilled in them. We are who we think we are. We all can be whatever we want to be. If I had convinced myself years ago, I would have been an author long before now. At age forty-nine, I am now finding out what my capacity is, as I am creating a reality. I can do whatever I want to do and be whatever I want to be—and you can also.

I give "hats off" to my daughter Millen for understanding that I wanted only what was best for her future. I also give myself a pat on the back for being a great mother who never gave up on her child and always set the best examples!

For any young adult reading this book, I encourage you to listen to your parents since they have only your best interest at heart, and to parents who have done their very best, remember this, "Moral values taught are those that are remembered."

Hang in there and
never give up!

Growth and Expansion of Mama's Dream

Years passed and Mama Dip's Kitchen was a still a success. Because of the many requests that she received from the community, Mama decided to write a cookbook. By this time, Mama had been writing down her recipes for a few years. Getting the hundreds of recipes out of her head was a tough job for Mama. As fast as she wrote recipes down they were typed. Even though she was busy working most of the time, she managed to jot them down, sometimes during the day and sometimes in the evening after she got home late from work. She was often writing late into the night.

I was excited about helping Mama with her cookbook. I didn't realize until after she began how much hard work would be involved. With a pencil she wrote her recipes on single sheets of notebook paper, and sometimes she used spiral notebooks, which were often stained when she occasionally got food on them. The spiral notebook was her favorite one to use, since she could always find what recipe she would be looking for without searching for pages all over the house. In order for me to read the stained pages so that I could type them, I had to hold them up to the light, so that I could see clearly what was written. It was not as difficult for me to type her recipes as it was to read Mama's handwriting. I read them, while scratching my head and thinking at the same time. Being used to reading recipes, I usually knew what she meant, but some of it I just couldn't figure out. All kinds of thoughts were going through my mind while typing, which included the struggle I had making the custom menus for her restaurant. It seemed like I managed to be around every time something needed to be typed. At the same time I needed to concentrate or else the process would be slow and difficult. Many family members helped and some friends of Mama's. It seemed as if everybody "kin" to her was helping. No matter how hard we worked at the restaurant, Mama continued to write recipes and we typed. Finally the recipes were given to UNC Press who had offered several years earlier to publish Mama's cookbook. I was happy when the recipes were out of our hands.

Bon and Lane had moved back to Chapel Hill from Atlanta, and Joe moved back from Louisville, Kentucky. Now all of the family except Bill worked at Mama's restaurant. Everybody who knew about Mama's restaurant was telling someone else who didn't know. Folks were coming from everywhere and lines formed out the door every day. My brothers, sisters, and I would say to Mama, "You need to start looking for a bigger place." But there was no place in town that Mama could expand her restaurant and still be located in an area where her customers could easily find "Dip's." We also said to Mama, "It's okay to move from this street— people will come for your food no matter where we are as long as we are in Chapel Hill."

Mama didn't think that moving her business away from the downtown district would be using good judgment.

ANNETTE COUNCIL

PHOTOS BY
TIFFANY PRATHER

Joe

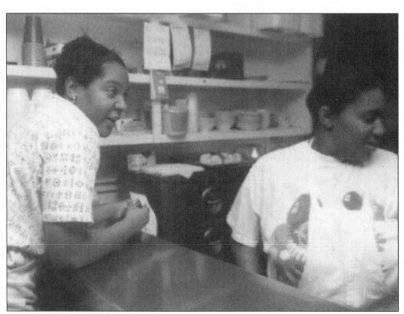

Lane and Sherry taking a break

170

Lane in first restaurant kitchen

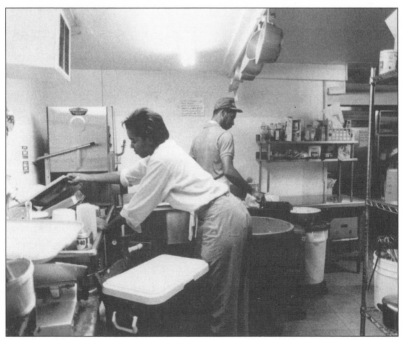

Spring and Joe   PHOTOS BY TIFFANY PRATHER

171

Consequently, she stayed at 405 West Rosemary Street. This meant that we were going to have to hang on a little longer and help her find a building in town. We all were thinking, "Where in the world could Mama possibly be thinking about moving to in Chapel Hill near where she was currently located?" In the meantime while all this pondering and thinking was going on, the restaurant continued to be packed with customers. The more people came to eat—the smaller the kitchen seemed to get. Mama had already tripled the seating in the dining area after she rented the other side of the building, but the kitchen didn't even double in size.

Even though the kitchen remained small we had to "make do." No one could be standing at the table when the oven door was open because it took up all the space in between. Lane and I prepared an unbelievable number of orders for breakfast on weekends. This was incredible for us and sometimes it got to the point where it seemed impossible in the tiny kitchen. We only had one grill and a toaster that took two slices of bread at a time. When we were busy, we'd juggle from continuously toasting bread to cooking more grits, hash browns, sausage, salmon croquettes and bacon. Some days I thought I was going to go out of my mind. Keeping up with the demand for breakfast meals became more difficult as the business grew. I miss the old restaurant, but I won't ever miss that damn kitchen!

Most of the equipment used in the restaurant was ancient—it was already there when mama moved in the building. Often our duties were difficult and required unnecessary work just to get the job done. I hated the old coffee pot because we always ran out of coffee in the middle of breakfast rush hour. The brew process on the old machine took thirty minutes to produce about ninety cups of coffee. The waitresses had to tote water in one of the pots used for cooking collard greens and brewing tea bags since we had to share them with the kitchen staff. The cook would sometimes rush and use the pot before it was used to make tea, so that she could complete her job before lunchtime. We constantly hustled and bustled about the kitchen bumping into each other. Sometimes it was a job just to move around inside the restaurant. My sisters and I begged Mama to buy a new coffee pot and tea urns. She wasn't about to purchase anything until she was ready, no matter what we thought. Often when we saw the need, Mama didn't. Eventually, she bought a new drip coffee machine, a new tea urn, and an automatic dishwasher. By this time the wait staff was practically jumping up and down with excitement, because they knew what it was like hustling around trying to keep up with the demand. Mama was not shy about telling us whose restaurant it was. As a result, we constantly had to learn to "make do" with what we had, despite the inconvenience, and most of the time our opinions were not considered. Now I understand why Mama ran her business the way she did. This experience has definitely taught me how to become a better leader. I now use our mistakes and successes to grow as an individual and to share with others how to improve their business concepts. In spite of our growing pains, business continued to prosper.

The notoriety of Mama Dip's Kitchen brought television stations, radio stations, newspapers, and magazine critics as well as patrons coming to experience the "comfort foods" of traditional country cooking. "Word of mouth" has always been Mama's best form of advertisement. When customers come to "Dip's," some of them ordered a vegetable plate, which included four fresh vegetables with a side of fresh baked homemade bread. The taste and atmosphere is "down home."

Customers could not believe that they were actually out at a restaurant, eating a meal that brought back their memories and the flavor that they were accustomed to growing up.

Mama's recipes are the kind of meals southerners ate during holidays or anytime at your grandmother's house. This is what Mama wanted to continue and making sure that the real traditions of America, when it came down to family, wouldn't be forgotten. She believed that one of the family traditions was at dinner time. When the entire family sat down at the dining room table to eat, it was understood that the grace was said. This is the grace that Mama taught her children:

God is great.
God is good.
And we thank Him for our food.
By our hands, may we be fed.
Thank you Lord for our daily bread.
Amen

No one ever said, "I don't want this or that," because everybody's plate was served with the same thing. Everyone ate and had fun talking about issues, or whatever happened that they wanted to talk about. After dinner, dessert was served, and, in our family, without a delay dishes were washed and each of us knew whose turn it was.

People nowadays have gotten to the place where they claim that they don't have enough time to prepare meals. When we get away from family traditions, our children lose the meaning of "family." At Mama's restaurant she decided to take advantage of the demand for "take home" traditional family-style meals. Her mission was grabbing the attention of families, bringing them closer together to build stronger communities. Everything that I experienced with my family growing up was about family and community. Later on Mama Dip's Kitchen contracted with Orange County in North Carolina for its "Meals on Wheels" program. The staff and the recipients of her meals were very pleased. The elderly folks were extremely glad to sample her food—Mama's special southern flavor satisfied their spirits. Because of Mama I knew some of them were healed from their illness. In addition, Mama started delivering dinner plates around town to the sick and shut-in folks that she had known for many years. To those who were bed-ridden she'd take some "pot liquor" from the cooked vegetables and broth that was made from the juice she had prepared for her chicken and dumplings.

One day a customer came in the restaurant to order some food for her husband who was hospitalized with a serious illness. She wanted to take him some "comfort food." The lady ordered chicken and dumplings and I said to her, "I will be glad to ask Mama to make him some broth for you; it will only take about ten minutes." "Okay," she said. Mama "whipped" up some chicken broth, and I packaged it to go. The lady was eager and excited to get the broth especially since Mama had taken the time to make it especially for her husband.

A few days later the lady came back to the restaurant to let us know that her husband had sat up in bed and he asked to sit in a chair, after weeks of being bound to a hospital bed. I smiled, Mama smiled, and the lady smiled as our hearts were touched with the thought of being able to make an ailing person feel better. It was nothing extra for Mama to do this because it was a part of her job description as a community activist. She often says, "I went into business to make people feel better through their bellies and hearts."

Mama decided that she wanted to start making her BBQ sauce to sell in jars at the restaurant and in other retail stores around the Triangle area. The State Department approved her restaurant facility to process her BBQ sauce and our poppy seed dressing recipes. Late into the night during non-business hours, Mama, along with Joe and Spring, prepared for processing. They ran the caps and jars though the dishwashing machine. The old fashioned Mason jars were sixteen ounces and each was hand poured with the BBQ sauce and dressing. The most difficult part of the entire process was attaching the "crack and peel labels" to the jars. It was tricky applying the labels in the same place on both sides of all of the jars, but we managed as we always have. Specialty stores around the Chapel Hill area began carrying "Mama Dip's" BBQ sauce and dressing. The products became a hit, especially when we participated in food demonstrations at stores, giving potential buyers an opportunity to sample them.

As a result we started selling large quantities. It did not take long for the demand to overwhelm our production routine, so we decided to find a manufacturing plant to help. We consulted the State Agriculture Department, which was the source of our much needed information, and they recommended several plants that could produce our products.

I contacted several plants and decided to schedule site visits with Mama to discuss production possibilities. The first plant we visited seemed a little busy for our scheduled time frame. We decided the next day to drive to Louisburg, North Carolina. This company seemed more qualified to continue with the consistency of Mama's recipes that she worked hard to achieve for many years. At this time I took vacation time from my government job to accompany Mama for this milestone.

Mama and I arrived at the processing plant early one morning, discussing with the staff her recipe, along with the type of jars, sealers, and labeling to be used. We were recommended printing and freight companies that the bottling company had used for many years for their business. After discussing all the specifics we headed downstairs to take a tour of the plant. It seemed that we were on our way to "showcasing" our first products for volume retail sales and I was ecstatic. Another big step was about to take place and we knew that our current customers would become buyers of these products.

About a month later production began. Labels were made and shipped to the manufacturer. We were there to be a part of the processing of the initial batch to insure quality control. As we walked through the front door there were employees wearing light blue hair restraints; Mama and I had to wear them also.

I was amazed at the machinery—I had never experienced watching a production line. The company had taken Mama's recipe and multiplied it about ten times to create a huge batch in a kettle that stood in the middle of the floor in their kitchen room. We watched as each bottle stopped at the hose that precisely filled each jar—then the jars moved along the conveyer belt where a lid was attached. Afterwards, the jar was sprayed with water to remove any excess contents off the outside. The labels were the last thing applied as the jars were sent down to the end of the processing line to be packed into twelve jar capacity cardboard boxes. The boxes were loaded onto a fork lift and sent on their way to be wrapped in plastic and put on a pallet for delivery.

Stefanie Bell

Spring

Register scene: Dip and Shawna

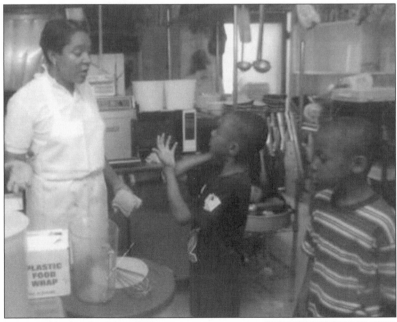

Lane working and raising children   PHOTOS BY TIFFANY PRATHER

Even though Mama was busy creating products, she still had relocating her restaurant in the back of her mind. She decided to design and build her own restaurant from the ground up—just as Grandpa had. The purpose of Mama's expansion was to create more seats and a spacious working environment for the kitchen. We worked for twenty-three years in her old restaurant building, pacing the floor around each other and most of the time bumping into each other. A new restaurant would also create more jobs for our community.

Mama purchased from her landlord two lots of property across the street from the existing restaurant. There was a vacant house sitting on the property that once housed the Internationalist bookstore. The bookstore sold rare books of many cultures and religious beliefs. With the anticipation of a loan from the Small Business Administration, Mama waited for her loan to be approved. The process took weeks of agonizing over red tape and paper work. Finally the loan was approved.

Mama was a very successful woman and my family thought that she had proven herself. My grandparents, Daddy and Mama had created hundreds of jobs for their community as well as property and sales tax dollars for the county and state that added to the budgets of these organizations. "Why was there so much hassle and what was the risk?" My family had proven that we were successful. "What else was it that we had to prove?" Certainly we could build and run a successful business—we proved that. The loan was approved with a local bank along with a second one being financed through the Small Business Administration. Mama was now prepared for her restaurant's expansion.

The architect drew plans and they were examined many times by my family before Mama came to a decision on the

Old house on restaurant property, torn down

type of building she wanted. The old Internationalist bookstore was torn apart piece by piece. Most of the house was
salvaged for recycling and it was used to help rebuild communities. Days went by and my family watched as the house was
taken down. Carefully, plank by plank, window by window,
and door by door. The house disappeared and the rubbish
was taken away.

The time had come for the foundation to be laid for Mama
Dip's new restaurant. The next day when I came to work I saw
sticks coming out of the ground. I took a walk across the street
to see what was going on. It was the beginning of the foundation. My spirit started to race inside of me as my heart felt
emotions that consumed me. I thought, "My family is about
to experience a dream come true." All those days sweating at
the old Dip's, bumping into each other, were about to become
history. "Oh, Wow!" I said with my hand covering my mouth

with excitement. I looked up to the sky and said, "Thank you, Jesus! Mama said it's going to get better." It took about a year for the new restaurant to be completed.

The finishing touches were near completion when I decided to walk across the street to take a look as I had done many times before. When I stepped on the porch, I started to have this odd feeling. I kept walking and opened the door at the front of the building. I went inside to take a look at the basic formation of what was to become another one of Mama's dreams. I froze in my steps because of how amazed I was at what I was really seeing. I grabbed my face and I started to cry with joy and happiness. I was feeling this kind of joy because I knew how long my family had struggled to get to the place where we are today. Praise God for giving Mama the vision, allowing her children to be a part of her success, and my brothers, sisters, and me for hanging in there with her.

The new restaurant was completed in January of 1999. The business only closed for a few weeks as my family and some of the employees moved utensils, food, and small equipment across the street. Dollies were filled with anything and everything, back and forth across Rosemary Street until everything was moved. While some employees were moving things, others were decorating the many bare walls.

The restaurant was built with two separate dining areas. The smaller dining area was decorated with the tables and chairs along with everything else from the old restaurant. This gave the room the same old rustic feel for some of our life-time customers. The lobby was decorated with plaques, framed newspaper articles, and framed pictures of scenes from the old building. The country porch was also decorated with the remaining tables and chairs along with the checkered brown and white tablecloths. Clay pots were filled with flowers to complete the porch scene along with ceiling fans.

My family was very pleased with the results of our new restaurant. We also wanted our customers to feel as comfortable with our new building as they had at the old building. Some customers told Mama that they would miss the atmosphere and how much they loved the old building. By this time we were approaching our 24th year at Mama Dip's Kitchen. A grand opening was set at the end of January and invitations were mailed inviting the public to come and sample our menu. People from all walks of life gathered at our new restaurant to greet and congratulate my family. Several newspaper editorial staffs, town officials, and bank officials attended the ceremony. The grand opening was successful and the time had come to open for real business.

It was coming down to the wire and Mama was eager to get the new restaurant opened. On February 1, 1999, Mama Dip's was opened for business with a new look, more seating, and most of all a bigger kitchen. On opening day the line was out the door and down the sidewalk. Mama anticipated more business, but she had no idea that customers would mob us. I dropped by on my lunch break to see how things were going. Lane asked me to come back after work to help them out; the look on her face was that of sheer desperation. I had no idea that they were packed all day long. The restaurant needed my help and that's where I went after I got off my day job. Things were very busy for months and I worked every day after work and on weekends.

Mama's cookbook was completed a year later and was on sale before the holidays in 2000. The publicity of the new restaurant and the new cookbook generated new customers from around North Carolina, and some came from other states. Mama was now a self-taught "dump" cook, owner of a successful minority woman-owned business, community activist, author, and most of all a great cook!

During this year, Roy, my cousin who became my brother, passed away due to kidney failure. At the time of his demise he was two years away from retirement after thirty years with the school system. He had continued to teach high school in Hyde County where he later became an assistant principal with the North Carolina public school system. Our family mourned his death, but we knew that Roy's work here on earth had been completed according to God's sovereign will.

His wife Nancy, along with his two sons, made arrangements to bring his body back to Chapel Hill. My family was grateful for the kind thoughts of his wife so that Roy could join other family members buried at the cemetery at Hamlet Chapel—his home church.

Roy's colleagues came from throughout the state to pay final respects to him. His body lay in state at Bynum-Weaver funeral home. This was the second time that we experienced a family member's death. I truly miss my brother. I love you, Roy!

Build your team.
You won't get
there alone.

The Process
of Giving Back

My family's lives have always been geared toward community involvement. We observed our surroundings, and doing so allowed us to understand the needs of others. We learned early on in life that our goals would be to prepare ourselves for opportunities. Many people have learned from us and have often asked questions and for assistance. There was never a day that went by without my family planning to give back, even when we didn't have much. Our neighborhood consisted of a church, gas station, grocery store, barber shop, beauty parlor, pool hall, and a funeral home. My grandparents', Daddy's, and Mama's businesses are what completed the neighborhood that my family grew up in. My family is well-known in our community, and we have demonstrated that no matter what we've encountered, there is light at the end of the tunnel.

One day when I grasped the handle of the front door at the restaurant, I noticed there were three people behind the cash register. I walked by with my head turned to watch two social workers teach a handicapped new employee how to use the register. She was five feet tall and walked with one arm slightly bent and stiff. She dragged her one of her legs that was also stiff as she walked. She wore a Jeri-Curl hairstyle that I hadn't seen in years, but I assumed it was perfect for her since she had limited use of her hands. Her name was Joanna. She had been a healthy fifty-seven year old and a member on the community softball team in her town about twenty minutes away. Joanna loved to play softball and she could run fast with her short legs. She worked many years at a manufacturing company until the day she had a stroke. Joanna was not able to return to her job because of her disability. All she wanted was a chance to work again, but she was beginning to doubt that a job was available that she could do. "If only somebody would give me a chance. I have been taken around to many businesses, but nobody will hire me." Joanna had no idea that the social workers had spoken to "Mama Dip."

Mama's community involvement helped her to understand people with disabilities. She felt that there was something that Joanna could do at her restaurant that wouldn't require a lot of movement. Joanna had a need and Mama's need was to continue to help build her community. Mama knew that if she helped Joanna, she was creating something concrete to the foundational growth of Chapel Hill.

Everyday Joanna made her way to work, driving in her dented beige Valiant. She'd pull up in the only handicap parking space, and wobble with her cane one little tiny step at a time. It took her about ten minutes to get inside once she was out of her car. She never had much of a smile, but she was excited about her new job, and eager to help out in other areas of the restaurant if she was needed.

I admired Joanna because she was a go-getter. She was a strong woman and nothing was going to stop her from working. "I thank you Mama Dip, and your family, for giving me a chance," she always said to my family. I assured her that if anyone gave her a chance, it would definitely be my mama. Helping others was the life that Mama dreamed about, and Joanna was no exception to her rule.

Our business is approached by many types of organizations seeking donations. One of the most heart-felt feelings of giving back to our community is with the Chapel Hill/ Carrboro School System vocational educational program. This program is geared toward high school students with learning disabilities. Throughout the school year students are dropped off by school buses in the morning. They come to the restaurant once a week to participate in our training program. They learn how to become productive citizens in the work place. They are first taught how to sanitize their hands. The restaurant staff demonstrates to their counselors how the different types of jobs are done. Then they are taught by their counselors how to wrap silverware, stack glasses, clean tables and chairs. Despite the disabilities of some of the students, all of them were able to learn.

We participate in numerous food-tasting shows. A Tasteful Affair is sponsored by the Ronald McDonald house and is held every year in October. This event is a first class affair with food samplings from restaurants in the surrounding Triangle area. Tables are prepared with white tablecloths for each restaurant and the room is decorated with fall colors. There were giant chandeliers hanging from the ceiling and shining down on the beautifully decorated tables.

Each restaurant prepares food to be displayed and served as samples from its menu. Tickets are sold in advance and each ticket holder comes to sample, mingle, and have fun for two enjoyable hours. The money raised goes toward living quarters for out-of-town families who have severely sick children hospitalized at UNC Hospital. This allows these family members to be close to their loved ones. Mama Dip's continues to participate in this event and has been part of this program for ten years.

Mama Dip's also participates with the program Project Graduation. This non-profit organization began in the Chapel Hill-Carrboro area in 1993, initiated by a small but determined group of students, parents, and school personnel. The vision was to start a yearly tradition for the high school, providing a safe, drug and alcohol free celebration following graduation. They wanted a student-driven event so that students would attend. They also wanted it to be free for all graduating seniors. The community responded generously and has continued to do so year after year. This tradition continues, now in its 13th year, with thousands of hours of effort by hundreds of volunteers and the generous support of numerous individuals and businesses like Mama Dip's from the community.

Our largest project is the Community Dinner held annually in February. This event celebrates Orange County's cultural diversity and encourages friendship, and most of all learning the culture of a stranger. Their motto is "Sit down with a stranger, walk away with a friend." Truly, this motto speaks for itself. Tickets for the event are sold through the sponsored businesses. The prices of the tickets are nominal. This is not a fundraising event, but an awareness raising event. Monetary donations received go toward those who cannot afford to purchase a ticket. The sponsoring committee encourages those who cannot afford a ticket to come and have dinner on them. This is the kind of neighborhood involvement that aids in building stronger communities.

The food contributors are of many cultures and so are the more than 500 hungry dinner-goers waiting in line for his or her chance to indulge. There is a team of volunteers on hand to help serve the crowd. Mama Dip's has been the main course contributor for the seven years since it began. This event suited Mama well. This is what she preached all of her life. She wants everyone to understand how important it is to socialize with your community and to remember real family traditions learned from our heritage. We all know that this is what builds stronger families that make great communities in America. Mama Dip's Kitchen won the neighbor award for participating in this event from the North Carolina Restaurant Association where the restaurant is a member.

Music and entertainment enhances the evening. The dancing sound and the beat of percussion drums move the crowd to foot tapping as the bands play. There is also an assortment of entertainment of different cultures.

RSVVP and the Interfaith Council for Social Services meet the basic needs of individuals and families and help them achieve their goals. Every year in November, a day is set aside for restaurants in the area to donate ten percent of their proceeds to feed the hungry. During the months before, participating restaurants are advertised in local newspapers, and on radio stations and television. Weeks before, the table tents are distributed to restaurants to advertise to their customers. The community really comes out on this day to participate as restaurants are steadily busy. Making a difference for the hungry while you enjoy your favorite meal is a favorite among those who participate.

The one thing that my family never lacks is food, and it is the least thing that we can do. RSVVP reminds me of when I was a young girl having to eat my vegetables. Mama was right; someone would have loved to eat what I didn't want. I am pleased that Mama Dip's Kitchen is a part of this event.

It is important to our legacy that we give back to the community. Giving is not measured—it's the thought. Mama's restaurant also donates gift certificates and gift baskets filled with our delicious products to non-profit organizations. Most of these items are used in silent auctions. Donations from Mama Dip's Kitchen may not always be large, but we have learned that the small ones can make a difference too.

Give back. To whom much is given, much is required.

Daddy, My Friend to the End

J oe "Tight Rope" Council was my daddy, and after many years we became brother and sister in Christ. My siblings also grew closer to Daddy—he always came around to talk with us while we were working at the restaurant, after he got off from his pizza delivery job. Daddy had worked hard most of his life, and he was definitely not about to sit around doing nothing with the time he had left. He decided to keep busy after his retirement, since working gave him a chance to get out of the house and travel throughout the community where he could mingle.

Most of Daddy's friends had already passed away. He always spoke about how they sat around after retiring doing nothing. Daddy often said, "I will not sit around and waste away." He knew that there was something that he could do and stay busy. That's why he worked part-time after retiring.

The more I got to know my daddy, I noticed that he was a different man. For many years he hustled to make extra money aside from his regular job. His money-making strategies were to win and not to cheat someone out of their money—one being gambling. Many days and sometimes nights he ended up away from home, because he was constantly challenged by his friends to gamble. Now as I take a closer look at my daddy's life, I see him as a true "merchant" just like his parents. The reason my grandma saw so much of Grandpa was that their business was in their back yard—home was a few steps away. When Grandpa decided to call it a day it was time for bed. By then Grandma would be asleep and the next day is when she saw him.

"Here come Daddy!" I'd say loudly so that every one of my family members could hear me, and this time we said it in delight. Sure enough, it was him walking through the front doors at Mama Dip's wearing his blue and red delivery shirt. I greeted him, "What's up Daddy?" He'd always say, "Nothing much, I thank God for another day. I just got off work and wanted to stop by for a few minutes before I called it a day."

Then Daddy sat in the lobby making conversation with his family and sometimes the employees. He never stayed long—"I guess I'll be going on home now." Off he went driving his tan Mazda with a huge smile from the joy he experienced when he was around us. Daddy wasn't around our house that much when we were youngsters, but he began to enjoy his family as he began to age.

He lived in a retirement community—the building was secure and a comfortable place for him to call home. The rent was based on a sliding scale. Daddy knew most of the people who lived there because they were from Chapel Hill. He was happy and loved his home. Daddy "wore" his retirement well.

He and I began to have frequent conversations, and I could tell by his spirit that something profound had changed his heart. Every time we were together, whatever he said, I listened closely since he always spoke about the Gospel

According to John. His favorite verses were John 1:1, 3:16, 6:44, and 10:27. Daddy wasn't the friendliest person when I was growing up, but he allowed these verses to transform his life. He told me that the reason he spoke so much about these verses was that he felt it was his job as a Christian to pass along the good news. Daddy was now living a better life and he wanted to share it with his family and friends. He and I bonded and spent a lot of time together sharing our life changing experiences.

Daddy drove every Sunday morning about an hour away from Chapel Hill to attend church at Crossroads Community, a televised church service. He found out about the church while watching TV. David Bibby is the Pastor. Daddy called the church for directions and drove until he found where it was located in Carthrage, North Carolina. By this time, Daddy and I had become really good spiritual friends. We shared a lot of inspirational time together during the last few years of his life. As a young girl growing up, the only spirit that connected the two of us was the spirit that quickly picked my "butt" up off the floor to clean the house.

I can't say now that I wished Daddy had changed his life when I was a young girl, because he consumed himself with hustling to making a living. At that time God and church was the last thing on his mind. My brothers, sisters, and I had Mama who sent us to Sunday school, Bible school, and church. We also had Grandma looking out for our spiritual needs during the time my sisters and I were teaching her how to read. It was important to her that we went to Sunday school as well. She wanted us to learn about the Bible so that we could teach her. It tickled Grandma after Lane, Spring or I finished helping her read, because she felt that there was never a time that she hadn't learned something from us.

My brothers and sisters also saw how Daddy had changed his life. Daddy never spoke so we could hear him, since he still had a habit of gritting his teeth and puckering his lips, although he made every effort to speak clearly and we all enjoyed talking with him. He welcomed our conversations and took time to listen—something he never did when we were growing up.

Daddy was never at our neighborhood cookouts or family dinners, and most of the time he wasn't home when Thanksgiving and Christmas dinners were being served—since he was always hustling. Even though Daddy and Mama divorced, he was still a part of the family. There were many times when my siblings and I invited him to our family holiday meals. Finally, Daddy sat at our dinner table and many times he'd be the one who said the Grace.

I visited Daddy often and I enjoyed spending time with him. Many days when I visited he'd shuffle through his sermon tapes and we watched them together. Afterwards, he grabbed his Bible from his bookshelf, pointing out to me verses to discuss for our own Bible study. Years before, Daddy had not been like he was at this time, but I was very happy to see that he had changed his life. Later in life he more than welcomed church, understanding that Jesus Christ was the only way for him to live the rest of his life with peace and joy.

When I was employed with the local government, Daddy often stopped by my office to visit. We went from a "Daddy-Daughter" relationship to regular "lunch buddies." Even though Daddy lived alone he continued to cook complete meals for himself since he loved to cook. During my lunch breaks I'd sometimes go to his apartment to join him for his delicious meals.

During the winter Daddy made us three course hot meals. This was "dinner," as his parents called their lunch time meal. I remember one day he cooked a beef roast that was surrounded by diced potatoes, carrots, onions and smothered in its natural juices. The roast had simmered in the oven all morning. In addition to the roast he made macaroni and cheese casserole with extra cheese on top. I laughed when he made the same blowing sound, as if he was counting his money, when removing a pan from the oven. He also steamed cabbage seasoned with fatback, salt, and pepper. Daddy never made homemade biscuits, and he didn't have a problem popping open a can of flaky ready-made ones. After they were golden brown he'd split them open with a knife and put a small pat of butter inside each of them.

Daddy was diabetic; he didn't drink anything with sugar since it was important to him to maintain his diet to control his condition. He was considerate and thoughtful as he always asked me what I wanted to drink so that he could pick it up while he was shopping. During the times I spent with Daddy, I finally got a chance to find out who the kind-hearted man was that I grew up around. (He was just like my grandparents' dog, Peewee—a loud bark with no bite.) Every dinner with Daddy was a savored moment as we grew spiritually at the same time as developing a real father-daughter bond.

During the spring and summer, Daddy would go to the grocery store and buy sliced deli meats and cheese. By the time I arrived at his apartment he'd have a full sandwich bar spread along on the countertop of his tiny kitchen. My immediate reaction was, "WOW!"—just like when I discovered the toys under his bed for Christmas. There would be a variety of meats, cheese, lettuce and tomato, sliced onions, mayonnaise, mustard, and toasted hoagie buns.

I grabbed a plate, made my sandwich, and reached into the bag of BBQ chips (my favorite) for a handful. Daddy handed me a can of soda and then I'd get ice for my glass. Many days when it wasn't too hot we'd sit on his patio while soaking in the warm sun. I moaned after every bite. After dinner, Daddy had a huge watermelon sitting in the bottom of his refrigerator waiting for us to finish for dessert. He took a knife from the kitchen drawer, while I retrieved the watermelon and placed it on the counter. Daddy made a slit down the middle of the watermelon—hearing the cracking sound—then the two halves fell side by side as he held onto the edges. The fresh smell of home grown watermelon filled the kitchen. Before cutting a slice Daddy cut a small piece off the top and offered it to me. I grabbed it with my fingertips, with my other hand underneath my chin to catch the juice from dripping on the floor. When my teeth came into contact with the watermelon, I verbally expressed the delight, "Ummm, Ahhhhh, this is delicious—it's really sweet!" Daddy then sliced two pieces of the watermelon, one for me and one for him. Daddy's face lit up with his smile from "ear to ear." I could feel his spirit of happiness as he thought to himself, "I have my daughter here and we are having a blessed time."

I was never ready to leave Daddy's after lunch. With my belly tight and full, my eyes would get heavy. Sleep always wanted to take over after meals with him. Unfortunately, I had to return to work. Slowly I'd raised myself from his Lazy Boy recliner, moaning as I headed toward the door and down the hall to the elevator. Daddy followed me all the way downstairs to the front door, and we said our goodbyes. When I returned to work I could not keep from telling my co-workers about my lunch partnership with my daddy. When I described our lunches their mouths watered and they'd ask me to take them with me the next time.

I knew that I could not take everyone to his house, so I decided that I would cook a meal for my co-workers. Everyone contributed money to buy food. The next morning I used the kitchen in the fire department to start cooking the fresh green beans. I diced the white potatoes, fried the chicken, and made homemade buttermilk biscuits. I baked cupcakes from a yellow cake mix and diced fresh strawberries for shortcake. I picked strawberries from the strawberry patch along the country side where I stopped on the way home the day before. Fresh brewed iced tea topped off the meal. Everyone enjoyed the southern meal that I prepared. After other employees found out about our luncheon, they began begging me to do it again and include them the next time. Consequently, I found myself cooking once a month for co-workers. By this time, all I could think about was what I had learned from Daddy and Mama—sharing my talents with others. In this case, the talent was cooking—which I had also learned from them. I shared food with a few and ended up drawing a crowd. A crowd equals a community; it doesn't matter where you are.

Daddy decided to stop working his part-time job that he enjoyed so much. He seemed to feel dizzy sometimes. Daddy served his country in the United States Army during World War II. He retired from Bill's BBQ, and unfortunately he didn't have a lot of money. He walked away from the home that he worked very hard to build when he and Mama divorced. Daddy was independent and he never asked for assistance. Without my brothers, sisters, and me knowing, he had applied for food stamps. It was determined that he would only receive $10 a week. I was disappointed that Daddy took it upon himself to apply for this type of assistance without seeking assistance from his family. There was no need for him to inquire about assistance. Since he had done this on his own, I felt the need to pursue why he was offered this minimal amount even though his family was there to help him. He had worked over sixty years, served in the US Army, created hundreds of jobs, increased tax revenues for our state; and $10 was what Daddy was offered!

I telephoned the Social Services office in disappointment. I explained to the woman on the phone how Daddy deserved more. I asked her, "Why is it that foreign people come into this country and get more than my daddy, a citizen? It's a shame. Thanks for listening." She listened and understood my point, but she could not give him anything more. Any assistance is based on income and the number of people in a household. I was glad that Daddy turned down the food stamps—he didn't need them anyway. He was a good cook and he knew how to make a great meal out of a little of nothing, and, most of all, he had his family.

Every morning Daddy's routine was walking four laps around his apartment community—he loved to walk for exercise. Some days he walked over a mile to the restaurant, if the weather permitted. Daddy was almost eighty years old at this time. One day the staff from his community called Bon to let her know that Daddy hadn't taken his usual walk. They also informed her that Daddy was acting strange. Bon went to his house and found him wandering around as if he didn't know where he was. He refused to go to the hospital, but Bon didn't give up trying to make him understand that something was wrong.

After about three hours she finally got Daddy settled down and convinced him to go to the doctor. Bon took

Daddy to the emergency room at UNC hospital in Chapel Hill, since he seemed very irritated and confused. After several hours had passed, waiting and talking with my sister, he was ready to go. He got up and headed toward the exit. "Daddy you need to wait for the doctor." Bon told him. So he decided that he could wait a little longer.

Later, Daddy was taken to an examination room where several tests were ordered. The doctors decided to keep him overnight to do more testing and evaluations. His initial symptoms appeared that of Alzheimer's, but the doctors were not sure at the time what was causing Daddy to be confused. The next day x-rays showed that Daddy had a mass on his brain. A biopsy was the next step, and result of the biopsy was not good news.

My family were notified and had to meet with the doctors the next day to discuss the next step. The doctors found out that the mass on Daddy's brain was a tumor that covered most of his right lobe. This was the pressure that was causing him to act confused. They also stated that operating was out of the question and radiation was possible, but would cause great discomfort. The doctors informed us that it was possible that he would live for only three to six months. "Nooooooo!" we all agreed, "If Daddy is not going to live, he doesn't deserve to suffer in his last days." I couldn't bear to go in the room with the rest of my family and watch while the doctors gave Daddy the news. He needed strong faces at this time. I just couldn't seem to be there since I knew that I'd burst out into tears, so I decided to leave and go back to work.

A few days before this happened, Daddy had a birthday party in the lounge at his apartment and asked his family to attend. It seemed strange to me that he was inviting everybody to a party when he never cared about a birthday, Christmas, or any other kind of special events. Now he wanted to have a birthday party? Not Daddy, and besides, presents were out of the question. I can remember when there were times that it would be June before he took the time to open his Christmas presents, and many times we opened them for him, we'd say, "Here's your socks, Daddy."

Bon remembered Daddy leaving the lobby heading toward the elevator to go upstairs to his apartment to get the delicious BBQ he had made. "I'm going to get the BBQ," Daddy said, and off he went. After about fifteen minutes everyone was thinking, "Why is it taking him so long to come back?" He made it back though, without anyone going to find him. By then, we started putting the pieces together and Bon thought maybe this "wandering around" Daddy experienced all began at his party.

The next day the doctor said that Daddy would have to spend the rest of his life in an assisted living facility. This is not what Daddy wanted, but he couldn't go back to where he was living. Eventually, he wouldn't be able to take care of himself because his condition would become worse. All of this seemed so unreal. Daddy looked fine to me and all of a sudden he was terminally ill. In just a few days, Daddy went from living in his apartment to a room in the hospital, and then to a room in a rehabilitation facility as a terminally ill patient. This was Daddy's worst nightmare as his environment changed over a course of a mere three days.

My brothers, sisters, and I were going to make sure that he was taken out of the facility during the day so that he only stayed there to sleep. Daddy ate breakfast every morning and one of us was right there to pick him up. He was always ready, waiting to go so that he could spend the day away from an environment that he was not familiar with. When I picked him up we always went for a ride around town. We often stopped to get out of the car to walk. One day while Daddy and I were sitting on the wall near the UNC campus facing Franklin Street, he said, "I never thought that I would be lost in Chapel Hill." I thought, "He really is losing his memory." From driving to deliver food for Bill's BBQ all over UNC campus, around to all of the different job sites, driving the countryside, and delivering pizza, he could not even remember the most well-known street in Chapel Hill. I said, "I get lost sometimes too, Daddy, but not in Chapel Hill." Daddy chuckled and I laughed, then we finished our sodas and headed back to the car.

Sometimes, during the week, Daddy came with me to my office and hung out while I worked. He was going back and forth from his room with different family members and was able to do this for about two months. One day when I went to pick him up, he did not know who I was—I couldn't believe what had happened overnight. It looked like he woke up in the morning with the intention that someone was going to pick him up, because he was dressed, and I guess by the time I got there he had totally forgotten.

When I walked in his room, I said, "Are you ready to go Daddy?" He just stared into space reaching out for something I couldn't see, and I said again, "Are you ready to go Daddy?" He continued to walk around the room acting as if he was grabbing and reaching for something with his hands. I stayed for a little while hoping maybe he would notice me. He had no idea that I was there or what was going on that day. I left because I knew for a fact that his room was the best place for him just in case he needed medical attention, so I left and drove back home.

The next day after work I went back to the facility to see how Daddy was doing. When I got to his room he was lying in his bed elevated on his back and staring at the ceiling. The nurse said that this is what he had been doing all day. Daddy didn't seem to feel good that day. I walked closer toward him near his head so that he could see me. I noticed that his eyes were moving around and around as if they were out of control.

According to his nurse, Daddy was now blind due to the fact that the tumor had grown and had taken over the part of the brain that controlled his eyesight. I approached Daddy on his right side, bending over close to his face, and I said to him, "Daddy, are you okay?" All he could do was murmur "Uh-huh." I was relieved to get an answer from him. It seemed like all of a sudden this speaking spirit that I was used to hearing was now quiet. All I could see was the body that my daddy's spirit lived in for many years. My heart was with him and I knew that he was there, but I didn't feel that he knew that I was—maybe he did. I still ponder over this to this day hoping that he knew that I was there for him. Daddy was captured inside of his body with a quiet spirit. I could tell that he was alive, by the movement from his chest, but the rhythm from his heart beat was slowing down.

I can't imagine what this would be like for anyone who could not move, but could communicate only by spirit—realizing, that's all we have anyway. Daddy was in control of his spirit, but his flesh had taken over his physical life. The end of Daddy's life was near. It seemed that his flesh became more irritating since he was showing signs of becoming uncomfortable.

I didn't go to see Daddy for a couple of days after he became bedridden. I felt that my emotions had started to take control over my spirit. I was getting ready for work on this particular morning when the phone rang, and it was Bon. She was always at the facility very early in the morning to check on

Daddy before she went to work. She was calling all family members to let them know that his blood pressure had been extremely low throughout the night according to the his nurse. I whispered to myself, "Maybe things were about to change as the angel of death was on the way." I hurried to finish dressing without even thinking about whether I had time to comb my hair. I grabbed the curling iron and ran out the door, jumped into my car leaving Cary, driving up Interstate 40, trying my very best to make it to say "Goodbye."

I arrived in Chapel Hill about twenty-five minutes later and was caught at the first traffic light in town. This gave me a chance to call Daddy's room to let Bon know that I was around the corner. She told me that Daddy passed away shortly after we hung up the phone, about the time I was leaving home." Okay, I thought, "I am about to enter a room with a dead person lying in a bed, and it is my Daddy." As I approached the hallway that led to Daddy's room, I noticed that the door was closed. I knocked softly and continued inside, and there was Bon, the Chaplain, and a friend of Daddy's. He was lying on his back with his mouth open, just as he had been for the last couple of days, according to my family. I thought, "WOW, this is it; he is really gone from earth now!"

The man who fathered me, kept me fed, and clothed me had taken his last breath. Despite Daddy "hustling" he still taught me right from wrong, and was the person that I can say was not only my Daddy, but my best friend. The memories I treasure that he and I shared will be a part of my life that I will always remember. When I was growing up I thought my daddy was an extremely tough man, but when I became an adult and after we began to share our spiritual lives, things were different and amazingly better for the both of us.

I have the utmost admiration and respect for my daddy. His spirit will always be my spirit; God gave us this grace in order for us to bond. I say to you, Daddy, "God's will be done on earth."

This was the third time I'd lost an immediate family member. By this time, I began to wonder about my own mortality, and how I was going to die when my time came. When my family went to view Daddy's body I was somewhat hesitant, but I managed. While I entered the building, memories of our life together began to unfold. I am grateful that Daddy and I had a chance to spend quality time together the last few years of his life. I walked around the casket to look at his body. I noticed that he had a smile on his face—something I had never seen during the many times that my siblings and I visited Bynum-Weaver funeral home. "He is at peace," I thought.

There are times when I think about my daddy that I want to cry, but I have no tears. I know that he is in Heaven with our Heavenly Father. Daddy knew where he was going—no more tears, pain, or suffering. Daddy's spirit has been a part of me and will continue for the rest of my life. "I love you, Daddy!"

Know your purpose, and live by it.

The Recipe

Ingredients for Growth

Always have faith; it's going to get better.

Add more than enough of being a good listener;
honor the opinion of others.

Add as much as it takes of trying something new;
make what you have better.

Build your dream; let the legacy continue.

Educate yourself; it's the key to learning.

Always love what you do; others will love you for it.

It's okay to let them see you sweat; success is tough.

Give as much as it takes of believing in your dream;
it will come true.

Expect the unexpected; it's part of the race.

Always add more than enough of being a good steward;
do what you expect of others.

Bumps and bruises are OK; heal and move forward.

Build relationships; you will need them down the road.

You can never add too much of hanging in there;
never give up.

Build your team; you won't get there alone.

Give back; to whom much is given much is required.

Know your purpose, and live by it.

The Recipe—How to "Make it"

I pass "The Recipe" along to you as a suggestion in giving back from the challenging experiences that my family endured. I now say to you, learn how to "make it." Always keep "the recipe" close by you. Your memory is the safest place to store it. That's where I keep mine. It's important that you live your dream according to these ingredients. They are the keys to becoming successful.

On your journey don't forget about balance; it creates joy and happiness. Understand what relaxation means along with the positive outcome that it will have on your body and your spirit. "The recipe" should include God's word, it has sustained me throughout the years, and allowed me to maintain my "sense of sanity" while writing this book.

My family became more successful than we could have ever imagined, and all we really wanted was to make a decent living. We allowed ourselves to use "the recipe" as our guide. The only time things didn't go well is when we consciously and sometimes unconsciously eliminated an ingredient, which weakened our foundation. After the ingredient was added back to "the recipe," things got back on track. That's what kept our hopes alive.

Where there is a will, there is a way—mostly there was something down the road that my family had a clear vision of and it was only a matter of taking the necessary steps to get there.

All of these ingredients are useful tools that will add strength to your foundation. Your foundation generates your future and will allow you to see your goals more clearly down the road. Once you begin to build, you will notice a difference resulting from using "the recipe." Try it, it works! "The recipe" is your own personal support system, intended to be used under all circumstances, which will encourage you to continue working toward your goals. Beware of cracks and leaks in your foundation, they are indications of missing ingredients. Listed below are the ingredients used in creating "the recipe" based on my family's living experiences.

Have faith; it's going to get better—Having faith is the easiest thing to do when things are dandy, but we must constantly learn from our challenges. Even though you think that you have done all of your homework, each day will bring something new. Whether it's good or bad, we must face it and deal with it.

I remember one day when an employee didn't show up for work, and I had to wash dishes for twelve hours. I thought to myself, "What fool would do this?" But after it was over, I was okay. Mama constantly preached that being tired is a state of mind. I just laughed. She was right for the first time, but after that—I was tired! You will never know what an employee's true talents are until they begin working. Training and trust is what I feel my family lacked, and this lack caused us to work much harder than necessary. Now when I look back, I clearly see and understand how some of the hours we worked could have been avoided, but we survived. We made mistakes and so will you. You must learn from them, correct them immediately, and move on. Mama's restaurant is a very successful business and every day is a challenge.

Be a good listener, honor the opinion of others—Don't be a know-it-all. Listen to suggestions, along with what is asked of you as a source to strengthen your foundation. Be careful about writing down your list of goals without understanding how to make them become a reality. Be specific and don't assume. Make sure that you not only hear, but also that you understand when you are in a conversation with someone— and vice versa, that they understand you. The worse thing anyone can do is to think that "I know." You may very well know, but sometimes someone else should be allowed to give their opinion. In many cases it will definitely have an impact on the outcome of decisions that you are about to make. Always be of good cheer and honor the opinions of others.

Try something new; make what you have better—Mama built her restaurant around traditions that incorporated family and community. Many of the traditional foods that she grew up eating, people don't take the time to make nowadays. She knew her job was to continue creating new recipes, using the old fashioned "dump" cooking method from basic meats, vegetables and dry goods. When someone told Mama that they did not like squash, she made squash casserole. Spinach was one of the main green vegetables I hated growing up. Mama now makes spinach casserole, and I can't seem to get enough. Tell "Dip" what you don't like and she can create a taste to make you rub your belly. Customers with children who would not eat vegetables at home asked their parents to take them to Mama Dip's. Mama not only satisfied the stomach and taste buds, her recipes satisfied the hearts and comforted the souls of customers. Whatever you do, keep on making what you have better.

      PS. I didn't say change what is already working.

Build your dream; let the legacy continue—Most of my adult life I was consumed with Mama's dream. I was excited that throughout the years of her struggles and hanging in there, she managed to persevere. Every day I woke to thoughts of Mama's dream. I spoke it, lived it, and I ate it.

      This book is my dream that I set on my "back burner" for many years. When I first considered writing this book, I became fearful. I had never written a book before and had no idea of how to begin. One day, I asked myself, "If I wrote a book where would I start?" After pondering for a few minutes, I began by writing what I am most familiar with, and that is my life. I could remember back to the early sixties. I just wrote. I didn't have a plan, and I continued to write. I decided to enroll in a conference where I learned how important it was to have a plan. After leaving the conference all I thought about was, "I am writing a book and I don't know the beginning or where it should end." On the way back home in the car, I sat in the back seat and birthed my dream. I wrote the order of my life in a table of contents form. As a result, this was now my plan and guide. One year later, I had a complete unedited manuscript that led me to self-publishing. Writing this book has been one of my most rewarding experiences. I am excited that now I have more dreams, and I plan to put all of them in print. Dream, Dream, Dream!

Educate yourself; it's the key to learning—Education is necessary for any dream to become a reality. It consists of gathering resources that support our goals in the process of our journey. Ever since I was in grade school I have always enjoyed going to the library. As an adult I began going to public libraries, and often I'll ask for assistance referencing my subject from the resource personnel who are always on duty. Don't feel intimidated because you don't know where to look. You don't have to know how to find what you are looking for, but you must know what it is that you are in search of.

I strongly believe in first hand information, written and published facts. Learn how to gather your own knowledge and share it. There's no easy way out when it comes to learning. The key to becoming successful at our dreams is by learning, and educating ourselves is how we obtain it.

Love what you do; others will love you for it—You must be passionate about your dream. If you are missing this ingredient, you must find something that you love to do, will work hard for, and will do for free. If you are like the members of my family then you are on the right track. Over the years, we worked countless hours day in and day out. My brothers, sisters, and I enjoyed cooking because it is what my grandparents, Daddy and Mama loved doing all of their lives. We also loved their different styles of cooking. Grandpa was a short-order cook, Daddy and Mama both were southern cooks. We learned how to cook as we mostly watched Mama creating recipes on a daily basis.

After I shared a dish that I made from Mama's recipes with my friends they always told me that they loved my cooking, just as Mama had been told for many years. People felt my mama through me. That's the powerful impact of loving what you do—it has a domino-effect. Over the years my family's love for cooking grew. Our skills improved and we all are grateful for what we have learned from our heritage.

It's okay to let them see you sweat; success is tough—Success is about a lot of time and a lot of hard work. Working for yourself will allow you to pick your hours, and you must decide whether or not eight hours is enough. If the lucky number is eight for you, stay on your day job, and that is where you will be until you decide that success is not a normal day.

My mama started her restaurant almost thirty years ago, in 1976, working from the time she opened her doors until it was time to close. Working all of the time was not exactly in her plans for herself and her children, but when customers want what you have, you have to be there for them. The word got around town and more people sought after "Dip's" food. Customers continued to come and pull on the restaurant doors even when we were closed. Mama thought that we should close on holidays to give everybody a break. Eventually, Mama decided that she had to be open whenever her customers wanted her food. It was not always about wanting to work hard, but for Mama it was about building relationships with her customers. She wanted them to continue to return to her restaurant and also to tell someone else about how good her food was. There was no way Mama was going to turn down customers when she knew that they were the reason for her going into business. Furthermore, they were going to make her business a success along with her recipes. If you remove this ingredient from "the recipe," remember trouble lies ahead.

Believe in your dream; it will come true—I was a young girl when my grandparents built Bill's BBQ. I am sure they thought about opening a restaurant for quite some time. Grandpa's dream was to create his own BBQ sauce recipe and sell the best fried chicken in town. He didn't just have a dream; he did everything possible to make his restaurant become a reality.

After twenty years in business my grandparents retired and passed Bill's BBQ down to Daddy and Mama. Grandpa was not about to sell and he didn't want to go out of business. Because of his health he had to call it quits. He sold the building to the same realtor that rented Mama her space for Dip's Country Kitchen. Daddy and Mama were not happy with my grandparents selling their restaurant building. Anyway, my parents paid rent to the realtor and everything else was left at the restaurant for them to use. The recipes, menu, and employees were what my parents had to continue the operation of my grandparents' legacy.

Expect the unexpected; it's part of the race—Don't even try it— thinking it won't happen to you. It will! My family learned a lot about surprises along our journey. Expect the unexpected. We also found out that what happens is not necessarily what our expectations were. Most of the time what we got is what we expected. On occasions there was a surprise; as some would say "sh...t happens." Our expectations are what made our legacy a challenge, and the unexpected allowed us to adjust our goals. Always have a backup plan. Don't worry when the unexpected happens, that's where we learn by experience.

Be a good steward; do what you expect of others—Working in Mama's restaurant business required my family to learn every job. I was a server throughout my college years. I prepared breakfast, lunch, and dinner orders. I had office duties, I washed dishes, scrubbed pots and pans, mopped floors, cleaned toilets, strained grease from deep fat fryers, and carried trash to the dumpster. I could not possibly teach someone else to do any of these jobs if I hadn't done them myself. There is not a woman that loves their fingernails more than I do. I had to choose to do without them and concentrate on doing what was necessary to help my family feed the crowd. So, I say to all of you, learn every inch of your business. Employees come and go. You either know your business or let them walk out the door with all the knowledge when they quit. Don't ever be left hanging!

Bumps and bruises are okay; heal and keep on going— Healing from the bumps and bruises along our journey is what allowed my family to become successful. Some of our bumps and bruises were thoughts that came along with working with family. Most of our mental bruises were self inflicted. We learned that we must always find a way to turn negative thoughts into positive ones.

Some of my family's bumps and bruises were burn marks, cuts, and scrapes from the many years of hustling and bustling around in the restaurant without proper hand and arm protection. Make a list and be prepared to purchase all of your tools. We learned that despite the bumps and bruises we must heal and move forward.

Build relationships; you will need them down the road— People are the main resource of exposure to new ideas. Our blessings come through people. Build your knowledge with those other than yourself. Whatever type of business you own, it is the people who will make it a success along with your creative ideas. Build business relationships. Enroll in classes and seminars. Join organizations and become a member of groups that relate to your dream. Information is knowledge and knowledge is power. Most business people love to network. Don't be afraid. You probably know something that can help someone else. Becoming knowledgeable in the area of your dream is the key to making sound decisions. Sitting around huddled in your own little world is not good when there is a whole world waiting for you to approach it. Don't just meet people and grab a business card—get to know them.

Hang in there; never give up—No one told my family that this journey was going to be easy. My grandparents, Daddy, and Mama had nothing to lose. All they wanted was to make a good living so that they could take care of family. Why not pay yourself and set your own hours? As long as you are willing to work hard, going the extra mile, exceeding one hundred percent, the outcome will put a smile on your face. Business got really tough for my family many times throughout the years, but we continued to push forward and kept hope alive. We made the best of every bad situation. We had to—even though we were not consciously aware of it since we were always consumed with work. It's important to get help from experts when needed. If you don't, you will find yourself discussing your problems with people, and more than likely they won't be able to help you. Just tell God and he will see you through every situation. My family started out with only the tools that we needed, and Mama's recipes were what people fell in love with and wanted. There was no need for fancy dishes, utensils or candlelight. For the most part, all my family needed was for the sun to rise and shine—that's what made every meal special. Because of Mama, we all knew that there was a need for traditions.

Build your team; you won't get there alone—Mama knew when she opened Dip's Country Kitchen, she could not do it alone. She was blessed to have a large family. Everyone contributed in some way, small or large, toward the building of the business. Every job description from the accountant down to the dishwasher was important to her success. Appreciate all of your team members and never take anybody's job for granted. Employees work better when they know that they are appreciated. Your team does not have to include family members. Mama included her children because we had already learned the restaurant business from our legacy. We all were a step ahead of the game when Mama chose to fly solo.

Give back; to whom much is given much is required—When we succeed at our dreams, there are blessings that come along behind all the hard work and headaches. We can now gather the fruits from our labor. That's why I stated in my preface, when there is more than enough, remember where you came from. Make sure you give before the harvest comes. It's part of the process of receiving our blessings. My family gave when we didn't have much. My brothers, sisters, and I learned many years ago the meaning of giving. Mama taught us that giving isn't necessarily about money, or about prosperity. Because of success, my family generously donates food and our time. Don't ever leave out this ingredient; it's what got us from where we were.

Know your purpose, and live by it—I learned a lot from watching my daddy gradually deteriorate into eternity. With that being said, I feel, until we all understand that life is not all about people and material things, none of us will be able to enjoy life to its fullest. Life is a spiritual process. One day, when I was a teenager, while sitting in a chair, I thought, "If I had to discard all of my personal possessions including money and all I had left was my naked self, what would I have?" I would have my body and my spirit. My spirit is what makes me a living being and my body is where the spirit lives. When I look back over my life, considering the financial blessings of some people, I understand why people have setbacks. Physical things consume their minds and only satisfy them temporarily. When things are no longer available to them, they become angry and wonder what went wrong. When we focus and choose material things over what is spiritual, God's process for life seems to come to an end quickly, but the spirit lasts forever. I am also grateful to God that He gives each of us a choice to follow him. This has allowed me to understand and live according to what is spiritual. I am grateful that God gave me to my daddy and mama. They never put anything physical before any human being. Often people say to Mama, "You're famous, Mama Dip!" "I am?" she often replies. She's just Mama, and that's who she strives each day to be. She still drives around town in her little truck. She says, "I want everyone to know who I am, not my material possessions that surround me." In fact, I have learned from Mama that living is about knowing oneself.

Mama Dip and Spencer Christian, "Good Morning America"

Epilogue

When I first considered writing this book, I was lying across my bed pondering over the thought, "Could I really do this?" I thought about my family and myself for quite sometime before considering where I should begin. I began to write from scattered thoughts of my memories as a child and growing up.

My life was quite an experience even at a young age. Mama guided and made sure her children were well groomed. Both my parents worked a lot, and my siblings and I made the best of our time together. We sometimes scattered throughout our neighborhood seeking to find soda bottles to sell for pocket change. When my brothers, sisters, and I became teenagers we continued to learn how to "hustle," and make our own money. We made the best of our integration experience, making friends by selling candy, cookies, candy apples, and cinnamon toothpicks. It was important to us that we had money in our pockets, even as children and young adults. Daddy instilled in our family the value of money. He made every effort to make money even if he had to "hustle" to help Mama take care of our family.

Entertaining ourselves was our priority when money was not available. Even today when I approach a funeral home or attend a funeral it reminds me of how we dared each other to go inside the funeral home to look at a dead body. I often wonder if some of the families still have the guest book of the people that we paid final respects to. I am sure that our names are in many of them.

Our home was the place in the neighborhood where most kids came to hang out. Our neighbors knew that my family welcomed them all. It was Mama's food that drew most of the kids to our house, and on most weekends during the summer she grilled out. They knew that they could get a handful of cookies and a glass of Kool-Aid.

The legacy of Bill's BBQ paved the way for similar types of restaurant businesses for my family and others. Numerous family members took on the task to continue my grandparents' legacy after their deaths and after Daddy retired. Eventually, Bill's BBQ closed its doors, leaving the thought of the hot dogs, burgers, and boxed chicken dinners lingering in the minds of family members. Our grandparents paved the way to our beginning, and are the road map to where we are today.

During the twenty years my grandparents operated Bill's BBQ, I could not have imagined that their dream would have instilled business ethics and the desire that every one of my family members have today. I didn't realize that I had so much inside of me that I could express in words as part of the history of my family. For over twenty-five years my family worked hard and we had no idea that we were part of an opportunity to achieve such accomplishments—but we are grateful.

I have learned from my heritage that in order to succeed at turning your dream into a reality, you must identify your greatness—cultivate your desires so the light that shines inside of you will have an impact on your life, as well as the lives of others. You will definitely have to put a lot of hard work into it and winning is the key.

Mama's influence has had a definite impact on my life when I look back over the years, understanding that what I have learned has led me to where I am today. She taught me right from wrong, along with how to be a lady. However, over the years Daddy and I built a spiritual relationship, something that was missing when I was a young girl. He helped me to understand many verses in the Bible. At the end of Daddy's life it was important to him that all of his children understood his life, as he went from a hustler to a humble spiritual man. Throughout each of our lives, despite the struggles and challenges, my family hung onto the one thing that kept us bonded—and that is our legacy.

I am grateful to God because of who I am today. My experiences have been my teacher for forty-nine years. I will continue to work with my family, who have been my inspiration to hang in there for all of these years—what a challenge!

Now I live life always looking forward to a new day with my recipe from yesterday. I will move forward to the next stage. I am proud of my family for the contributions that our businesses have given back to society, and the impact that it has made on the lives of people in our community as well as in the hearts of those in other communities throughout the United States, Canada, Europe, and Africa.

Mama continues to operate her successful restaurant business, Mama Dip's Kitchen, Inc. in Chapel Hill, North Carolina. Yea-Yea, Joe, Lane, Spring, and I work for Mama at the restaurant. Norma operates her successful daycare, Little Teddies, Inc. in Chapel Hill. Bon operates her successful restaurant, Bon's Home Cooking, in Chapel Hill, and Bill operates his successful printing business, Image Solutions, in Charlotte, North Carolina.

I am blessed to have been able to savor the good things, overcome the difficult things, and understand the challenges that I have experienced in my life. Through it all, it has allowed me to consume and store in my heart the words that are contained in this book. For sure, I can now say, I have certainly learned a lot!

Glossary

Back-eye—surface burn unit/element of a stove

Boogieman—a monster created in your mind

Bottle Collecting—the act of picking up loose soda bottle off the ground

Black Wall Street—black businesses in a heavily populated black district

Country Butter—homemade churned butter

Creek Fish—fish trapped from streams and overflow of lakes and rivers

Chunk—throw rocks

Crinoline—starched laced undergarment

Chicken Box—a soft cardboard box that holds food

Chitterling—cooked hog intestines

Caught Hell—payed the price for being right or wrong

Cook-Out—food cooked outside

Dog Bread—fried cornbread

Down Home—the feeling of home

Dump Cooking—cooking without measuring

Fixin'—the act of doing or making

Flinch—to draw back with body

Food Spies—critics seeking to find outstanding restaurants

Hang Out—a favorite local spot to socialize

Hot Comb—a heated tool used to straighten kinky hair

Hard Headed—not a good listener, stubborn

Hustle—the process of making quick money

Jack Rocks—a game with a ball and rocks from the ground

Kin Folk—relatives

Makin' a Killin'—result of selling a lot

Neighborhood Bonding—building relationships within the community

Play Clothes—worn old clothes for play

Pocket Change—loose coins

Pot Liquor—juice from boiled vegetables

Raise Hell—the act of losing your temper

Row Houses—multiple attached houses in a neighborhood

Slop—food scraps fed to hogs

Sunday School—class taught at church

Sunday Clothes—clothes for church

Whuppin'—old fashioned beating